Tinsel and Tapas

Solo in Andalucia

In Search of Christmas

By Paula Rooney

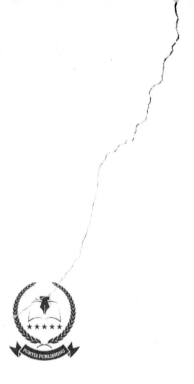

ISBN: 978-1-913822-90-3

Fortis Publishing
Kemp House
160 City Road
London
EC1V 2NX

DEDICATION

I dedicate this book to my family who made Christmas so special over the years, beginning when my mum laid the foundations of how to celebrate it all in my childhood right through to the traditions I have passed onto my own family.

I dedicate this to the tiny children who got excited with every gift they received as I watched them grow up into the adults they are now. Seeing your adult children buying gifts for each other that they have spent time choosing carefully, or even making, is heart-warming.

I also want to dedicate this book to everyone who is struggling with an empty nest at Christmas. It's not easy.

ACKNOWLEDGEMENTS

Thank you to my readers, every single one of you. Without readers, I couldn't carry on travelling and writing. Thank you to all the team at Fortis. Particularly Ken Scott for his never-ending support and everyone behind the scenes doing the jobs that I don't see.

To every single person I spoke to about the title, thank you. It was a struggle to agree on a suitable one. In the end, it was Ali Ward who actually thought of it, off the back of Ken's suggestion. It hasn't been easy trying to get the title to convey the content of the book but I think we have done it.

I am always grateful to Emily of Emily Charlotte Editorial, not only for doing a fantastic job editing the book but for being there in every aspect along the way.

A huge thank you to Kim Clark and Ray Livett for helping me out of a very stressful situation. I was – and still am – incredibly grateful for their kindness and willingness to help a complete stranger in their hour of need.

Finally, thank you to my family for letting me do my thing over Christmas.

About the Author

Paula Rooney was born in 1965 in Harlow, Essex, then spent several years in Ipswich, Suffolk before settling in St Austell, Cornwall in 2001 to raise her family.

Journaling holidays started with the first family break to Cornwall when she was ten, followed by a trip to Scotland and another back to Cornwall. When she was thirteen, her dad left the family for good, taking the car with him.

Then, three years later, her mum took them by bus, since she didn't drive, to holiday at a caravan park at Burnham-on-Sea. This might have ignited Paula's passion for travel and instilled a sense of adventure. If you don't have a car, you get a bus. If you don't know where you are, you look on a map.

This is Paula's third travelogue. Her first book, I Hope There's a Kettle in My Room, and her second book, Odd Poles and Baggy Trousers on the Camino de Santiago, are available on Amazon.

On her website, readers can see photos from her trips to complement her books, found at paularooneyauthor.co.uk

Contents.

Monday 18th December

I am on my way to Spain for Christmas and New Year. The train has just left St Austell station from Cornwall, and it all feels a bit surreal.

I'm not sure why, as this is my third solo trip, but I am shaking. I have packed everything and my flight isn't even until tomorrow morning, so I have plenty of time. Don't I? Yes, I know I do. So, why am I anxious?

Why am I even on a train, out of Cornwall, at Christmas time?

I watch Cornwall slip away from me out of the train window, feeling nervous. I am on my way to Bristol airport on a train and then a bus. I haven't taken my car because I will be away a month and I haven't booked a return flight.

I do know why I am leaving Cornwall and my family. The thought of having another bad Christmas has made me run away.

Whatever happens this year, whether it is good, bad or indifferent, it won't be like the last few years, and that's all I am trying to achieve.

I need to step away, re-assess and re-think Christmas. I need to try and understand what has gone wrong and see if it's possible to fix it. Or whether I need to just accept that Christmas is never going to be the same again.

When my children were small, Christmas was extremely important, a big highlight of the year. It was filled with excitement, anticipation and laughter and I could barely sleep on Christmas Eve, I was so excited.

Now, going forward, I need to think seriously about how I will celebrate Christmas. What traditions do I want to keep, and which ones do I want to throw away? Maybe I want to delete the season completely.

Because I don't want to go through the motions any more, and always end up disappointed on the 25th of December. I need to either do it better, or not at all.

So, right now – on this very train – I am avoiding a traditional English Christmas in favour of a Spanish adventure.

Already, with two life-changing solo trips behind me, this one will be all about experiencing a different December 25th, a different festive period in Spain. I could have chosen anywhere in the world, I just want to experience another culture.

But what's been wrong with my last few Christmases?

My children weren't there. It's that simple.

Christmas without my children doesn't feel like Christmas. And now, my children are all adults and doing their own thing, with my blessing, of course.

But, oh my, do I miss them.

I miss what Christmas used to be when we all lived in the same house, which will never happen again because they have their own lives, as they should. It did gradually evolve from the chaos of toddlers to teenagers and then adult children. I tried to hang on to the traditions, still making stockings and their advent calendars but it all gradually filtered out.

I can't return to those days, they are gone and it feels like a form of grief, which is a bit dramatic, but I do feel like I have lost something. I am not disappointed that they have all grown up and found their way in life, because that's great news and exactly what should happen.

I am just disappointed that I haven't adjusted to that, yet.

There are many stages to having children and they are often talked about. Relations warn you about the terrible twos, the stroppy teenagers, but I was never told about the pain of them leaving home. No one warned me that it was going to be the hardest part of having children. Letting them go and the pain of missing them.

So, here I am, with a packed suitcase and going to the Andalusian region of Spain, because I want to see how Christmas is done somewhere else.

On this train, there's a lady wrapping presents on the other side of the aisle with paper that looks like parcel paper, noisy and thick. She looks a bit stressed, obviously behind with her gift wrapping, maybe even meeting the person who the gift is for at the end of her journey. I won't be exchanging any gifts on Christmas Day, which might be strange, or liberating. I won't know until I am there, experiencing it.

I am wondering now if this was a sane idea or complete madness. Maybe that's where the anxiety is coming from.

But I do enjoy a train ride, watching the world go by out of the window. When it's time to change at Plymouth, the transition is smooth, just a hop across the platform. I take a seat on a different train and off we go again.

The thing about travel is it takes you slowly, further away from where you were. Each mile in this direction is a mile further away from home.

Which is scary, and very unsettling.

It might be why we all feel enormous relief when we get home after a holiday or trip away.

Even if we see faults in our lives, our home, our work, the struggles, it's still home and we love to return.

Once I arrive at Weston-super-Mare, I think about wandering around to explore as I haven't been here since I was a child. But it's such a dull, grey day that I don't fancy it, and the bus to Bristol Airport is due in ten minutes.

The journey takes an hour. It feels strange going to an airport when my flight is not until tomorrow but my accommodation is in walking distance to the terminal.

I buy a meal deal and snacks in the airport shop and walk the 15 minutes to my accommodation. Thankfully, I know where I'm going as I have stayed here before. When I get there, I make a cup of tea, sit on my single bed and chill.

This trip is quite different from my other two trips; I am

not interrailing or doing a very long walk.

In fact, I am travelling with only a small suitcase, so it definitely feels more like a holiday.

Over the last few months in preparation for this trip, I have booked hotels in Seville, Córdoba, Ronda and Málaga, which is much more planning than I usually do but, because it's Christmas, I felt I needed to secure accommodation. I have left enough room for flexibility and I haven't booked a flight home.

In my room for the night, I am so close to the airport that I can hear the planes taking off which is making me very excited now. I am so looking forward to my one day in Málaga and particularly looking forward to seeing the Christmas lights.

Perhaps a contradiction of sorts. But it's not that I don't like Christmas, I have absolutely loved it in the past. Maybe this trip will inspire me to love it again.

Tuesday 19th December

I fall asleep by 9.00 pm. but get woken at 2.00 am. and then 3.00 am. by the people opposite who didn't get the memo about being quiet for your neighbours as others are trying to sleep with early flights booked.

Then at 4.30 am., the man in the other room runs down the stairs and throws up in the car park, noisily like a cat with a furball.

Add to that the Christmas decorations hanging outside my window flashing like I'm at a disco for the night. Eventually, I do manage to sleep between the chaos and I wake up pleased that it hasn't dampened my enthusiasm – in a few hours, I'll be getting on a flight to Málaga.

After a 10-minute walk, I arrive at the airport a bit soggy, happy that my new raincoat has worked well and I got to use my suitcase cover that I picked up in TK Maxx, though my woolly hat is wet. Walking into the airport to the sound of festive music is a first for me.

When I was a child, we never left the house on Christmas Day. It was an important day, one that was very, very special and we all stayed in to play with our new toys. I couldn't have imagined doing anything else.

I lived an ordinary life in the 70's, where you rarely got treats unless it was your birthday or Christmas. So, Christmas Day was a day of being utterly spoiled with presents, gifts and food. My mum stocked up on special treats for the 25th but the night before we ate beans on toast, egg and chips or something simple. We had to wait patiently to eat all the special food, like crisps, nuts, dates, Quality Street, sweets in our stockings, and selection boxes. There was an abundance of it all which only got eaten then. It was a very special day and I had no desire to go out.

Even as an adult, I struggle with the idea of going out on Christmas Day, even if it's just to pick my mum up to join us. It feels wrong being the other side of the door.

I expect most people here at the airport are travelling home to their families but I am travelling away.

The flight was uneventful which is always good news and I read All my Mothers by Joanna Glen the whole journey. I have read it before but wanted to re-read it before I get to Córdoba where the story is set.

We all get off the plane, down the steps and straight onto the tarmac. I know it's a stupid thing to say but it always amazes me how a two-hour journey on a plane can take you somewhere so different. I left a grey, overcast, cold England and arrived in the sunshine with a Spanish blue sky and mountains in the distance. I love travelling. I love the change in scenery, the change in climate, the new smells, the possibilities.

I go straight through customs out of the airport and swiftly onto a bus into Málaga centre.

There, I put the Wi-Fi on and my hostel address in Google Maps. As I look out of the window, I already feel blessed. I love Malága so far, it's big and clean with shops lining the roads on the exit from the airport. I am so excited to see the rest of the city, my room and the Christmas lights later.

The street sign says it's 16 degrees outside but I am melting in my leggings and lace up trainers.

When it's time for my stop, I get off the bus and walk up a tree-lined avenue with lovely big buildings. All the while, I can hear birds making quite a racket. I stop and look up and, in the palm trees, there are lots of green parrots nesting and squawking. What a treat.

I love it here. I don't mind that I am leaving tomorrow as I have already decided that I would like to come back one day for a long weekend.

In front of me, Larios Street is pedestrianised with tall, elegant buildings on either side with two rows of big gold pillars spaced out the entire length of the street. Each has a huge gold angel balancing between them. Along these rows hang Christmas decorations, sparkling gold bits hanging and dancing in the light wind. It's quite phenomenal. I am stunned by the scale of it. There is so much gold glinting in the sun, it looks amazing against the blue Spanish sky.

Google Maps says that I am at my accommodation, Hostal Larios, so I look across through the decorations and see that, yes, there is my hostel in one of these large elegant buildings above the shops.

I pinch myself.

My single room has tall patio doors that open onto a miniature balcony, looking down over the decorations. I am now higher than the angels and I can see right up the street as they drift off into the distance.

I can't believe how lucky I am. I have literally struck gold with the hostel and this was €42.30 a night. That's probably on the high end for a hostel but so cheap for this view.

Inside, it's a tiny single room – literally a single bed, a thin wardrobe and a sink. The bathroom is across the landing. But I don't care where the bathroom is. This is more than I dreamed. The only thing that I really wanted to do in Málaga was to see the Christmas lights as I am only here for one night, and there they are right outside my bedroom window.

Sadly, there's no kettle – I have already asked at reception. The receptionist says there's hot water in the tap, but I know from experience that the tap is not hot enough and it doesn't make tea. My loose green tea won't sink unless the water is hot enough. Maybe I should have brought my travel kettle with me but I was conscious of space in my suitcase.

Looking ahead to tomorrow, I book a bus ticket online for my journey to Ronda and then I go out to explore.

I always feel more comfortable if I check out my onward journey beforehand, so I walk to the bus station and see how far it is so I can plan my timings for tomorrow.

Afterwards, I notice that the streets here have orange trees scattered about, which is unusual. Some have fallen onto the ground so I pick one up. They are really hard but must be ripe if they have fallen. The one I hold in my hand smells very strong, stronger than I have ever smelled before. Maybe they are Seville oranges? Which would make sense.

I wander around the old town with the tall, ornate buildings with shops underneath and the thin streets.

An indoor market is bustling and I'm pleased to see there are a couple of tapas bars. But I can't quite work out what is happening. It's a very busy market and people are drinking glasses of wine, leaning against the counter of the market stall, but the food looks raw. One lady has a plate of empty mussel shells. Perhaps they cook your order fresh or something.

The menu is hand-scrawled in messy, colourful writing on a white board. I can see Bollinger for €65 and Dom Pérignon (2013) for €280. Maybe they have forgotten the decimal points? Or maybe they haven't, I am not sure. I do know this isn't a posh restaurant to justify those prices, it's a market stall. The glasses are hanging up across the top and there is raw fish in the glass counter, like lobsters and big prawns.

I have no idea how to take part and I don't think I have the funds or even want any fish cooked for me. Plus 3.30 pm. is a bit early to drink Bollinger in a market.

So, instead I go to a brightly coloured fruit stall and buy a persimmon and a small, bobbly cucumber which is very similar to one we grew on the windowsill once. I keep exploring and find a Carrefour Express so buy a tub of guacamole, a bag of crisps and an Aquarius drink.

After taking photos of beautiful ornate, unusual-shaped buildings and the Christmas decorations, I return to my room and have a picnic, then return back outside to walk towards the sea, passing a whole row of pop-up stalls selling all sorts of tourist stuff along the promenade.

Along the way, I get distracted by some beautiful gardens and explore until I am standing at the Alcázar, a huge deep-walled fortress on the hill. Purple flowers bloom against the lovely stone walls and, again, the sun is shining, lighting up the exterior of the building.

I have no idea if you have to pay but decide to stop climbing and save this for another day as I am short of time now. From here, I can see down to the port.

At street level again, I keep walking towards the sea but glimpse an area full of orange trees so detour once more and take a wander. I have never seen so many orange trees in one spot, all the trees are full to bursting with oranges. There is also a little pond surrounded by ceramic decorations. It's quite lovely.

There are so many ripe oranges that the air is thick with a rich, citrusy smell. Squashed oranges scatter the floor and I find two that look whole and yummy so put them in my pocket. I hope I'm allowed to do that.

Satisfied with my forage, I cross the busy main road until I am surrounded by trees lining the path, beautiful palms and other trees, and lots of bird noise as well.

My feet are drawn in the direction of what looks like a huge pile of Lego bricks but, as I get closer, I see it's a big, transparent cube with painted blocks of green, yellow, red and blue. The sun catches the structure just right, lighting it up. It's quite beautiful for a square, simple design. I see a notice that says the coloured bricks are part of the Centre Pompidou Málaga. That makes sense, an art installation. Near it, the harbour is home two cruise ships and lots of posh superyachts against a background of mountains and industrial cranes.

A palm tree-lined avenue sits along the water's edge and I decide I am going to try and get down there for a walk. The lower level boasts lots of market huts and a huge Hard Rock Cafe.

I wander about, thinking of going back, when the cruise ship blasts its horn and I notice the water in the port moving.

Ooh, exciting.

I stand and watch. The ship takes quite a while to swing around and face the ocean. It's so dramatic and huge but I am not sure I would enjoy being trapped on a huge ship like that. It's one of those experiences that you would either love or hate, and by the time you set sail it's too late to change your mind. I would enjoy stopping at all the destinations I might not otherwise get to visit but I also know I would get frustrated with the timings and restrictions. Luckily, I can't afford it anyway, so it's not a problem.

Now, the sun's going down behind the mountains, leaving an orange glow in the sky. As I watch the rays fade, it's getting chilly.

While the ship slowly cruises out of the port, there are still lots of people wandering about, couples and families. The only difference to a summer's day is their clothes. They are darker, not brightly coloured summer wear like I'm used to in England. Here, it's mostly jackets and coats. Finally, I watch the MS Amadea leave us once and for all. It is quite impressive, but slow.

I walk down a handful of steps but, because I am still watching the sunset, I miss the last step and lose my balance. Luckily, I don't fall to the floor.

That shook me up. I could have broken something and I'm really grateful that I didn't fall. But I do feel jarred, and my back hurts a little.

Gosh, I hope I am OK, my back is a bit weak from having three children close together, pushing a double buggy up and down kerbs, and falling off the draining board years ago when I was washing the windows. Day One of my holidays and I could so easily have sprained something. I need to concentrate more.

I stroll back along the dark, tree-lined path and suddenly realise that I am out at night on my own.

I knew it would happen on this trip, as it gets dark so early in the winter. But it feels safe and I know I have thought this through. I have a sensible backpack – my Osprey one from my interrailing, choosing function over style – and I have the clasp done up across my chest, so it can't be taken from me easily. My waist bag is under my top with my phone and money in, which is zipped and out of sight.

Just common sense, really.

I don't want to have anything stolen so I will get into a routine where I always have my money and phone secured away.

After a short while and once I'm back near the buzz of people again, I stop and buy hot chestnuts from a stall and cross the main road with bright Christmas lights decorated above it.

As I get back to Larios Street, I hear the sound of music being piped into the street. Feliz Navidad is playing and the lights are dancing along too. The street is now packed with people watching, and singing to the music. It's a great atmosphere, such a happy, bouncy song with so many people enjoying it.

The tall, beautiful buildings are now illuminated by the lights and shine as gold as the decorations. It's far more impressive than I was hoping for, with the gold and bright lights dancing against the night sky. There are other Spanish songs being played that I don't recognise, but I enjoy it all.

I can't remember ever seeing music being played to Christmas lights before. My children's school, Bishop Bronescombe, used to do a brilliant firework display to music which was amazing. But I can't remember seeing lights dancing to Christmas songs like they do here. Being outdoors in mild weather helps with the happiness level as well, I think.

Strangely, all this still isn't giving me any festive feelings. Perhaps because I am not familiar with the songs and so they don't remind me of Christmas. Is that one of the clues? To get the Christmas feeling, you have to be reminded of Christmas? Maybe because it's so outdoorsy, it doesn't feel like it at all, although I have seen lights being switched on at home, especially when the children were young. Maybe it's because I don't know anyone here.

I continue exploring, admiring the decorations and taking photos, trying to capture it. At the end of the street, separated off in a square, I see a cylindrical gold tree which people can go inside, and I take even more photos. There's no actual tree though, just this gold pretend one.

I wander around the old town then on my way back to the hostel, I stop at a bakery and get two unusual cakes for tomorrow. One big, round flaky one with nuts on top, called a Coca de vidre and one that looks like rolled up pastry. This is my kind of cake shop, all pastry based with very little cream.

Back in my room, the lights look even more impressive as I can see all the way up the street from this height. I leave my balcony open and listen to the chatter and noise which is lovely.

I finish my guacamole and crisps, drink my Aquarius, and

have a couple of chestnuts.

At 8.00 pm. the music and light show starts again and I know I have the best spot in Málaga – I'm not joking. I can see all the lights and people below, hundreds of them, really well. They look up at me as if I am important; not one other person is on their balcony.

It's magical and I feel so lucky to have landed up here.

The air smells of churros and roasted chestnuts, happiness, and families.

After it's finished, I sit on my bed and upload some photos to Facebook, still listening to the hubbub below. A constant stream of activity hums outside my window but at 9.15 pm. I have to shut my balcony door. It's very nippy but I can still hear music.

For the last show at 10.00 pm., I slip my coat and shoes on to stand out there again and watch. Lots of people still mooch about and a long set of tables sits out with men around it playing a board game, possibly chess, I can't see from up here, it could be backgammon. Lovely to see, but they must be chilly sitting there. People are standing around looking at them with interest. It's not something I have ever seen in England, even on a sunny day, and certainly not at 10.00 pm. in the evening.

It's so outdoorsy here. I wasn't expecting that as it's still cold – not English cold, but there's a bite to the air.

I am now in bed facing my balcony and I have left the curtains open. It's noisy out there, the night air filled with conversations, laughter and people moving up and down the street, but I like it. There is a gold glow to the air.

I am shattered, it's been quite a day, and I have walked 2,2601 steps. But I will read until I can't read anymore. It won't be long. I have enjoyed Málaga.

Wednesday 20th December

It was such a comfy bed and I slept really well, but I can't have a cup of tea which is difficult. I hope there's a kettle at my next accommodation in Ronda.

I pack up my stuff and eat a pastry thing that I bought yesterday and then leave. It only takes 20 minutes to walk to the bus station. Waiting for the lights to change at a dual carriageway, I notice a man cutting grass on a verge between the lanes of traffic. I don't think I have ever seen Christmas decorations and grass cutting at the same time. The air is filled with a rich freshly-cut grass smell. Like a summer's day but it's December 20th.

At the bus station, I'm a little nervous because my bus isn't up on the screen yet. I have never bought a bus ticket online before; I usually buy one at the bus stop.

I got myself here with my paper map that the hostel gave me, which is better than Google Maps and I didn't need to walk around with my phone out. Losing it would be a nightmare, so I will try paper maps as much as I can and, to be honest, they make more sense to me.

Ahh, my bus is up there on the screen now for 12.30 pm. to Ronda at bus stop 31.

So while I wait to get on the bus, I reflect on what I've thought of Málaga? Firstly, I know I want to come back because I've only scratched the surface. This is a place to enjoy with someone else, to sit in an outdoor cafe, to people-watch, and enjoy a meal.

I know the Christmas lights were phenomenal and added something, but I feel confident that Málaga would be as good at a different time of the year too. The Alcázar needs to be explored as well. The harbour a bit more, and a walk along the seafront. I didn't see any beaches here but I expect there are some. I was only in the port and obviously, with huge cruise ships moving about, that's not the place to swim.

I have felt safe here and the people seemed calm. There are

a lot of dapper men and women here who look in the mirror a lot. Some well-made clothes being shown off, shiny shoes and smart clothes, as well as normal people with jeans, t-shirts and normal shoes.

Málaga is a bit rough around the edges. It's not all old town and beautiful buildings, it's a working town, an historical town and a seaside resort.

The bus ticket worked. It still amazes me that you can sit on your bed, book a bus ticket, and get on a bus without communicating with any human at all. It is convenient but I am not sure I like it.

I hate leaving my case in the big hole under the bus so, predictably, I sit where I can see the door opening and hope no one runs away with all my belongings. And at 12.30 pm., we leave La estación de Málaga. What a whirlwind.

I look forward to the views out of the window. I am familiar with northern Spain, having walked 500 miles of it which still seems unbelievable. What will southern Spain's countryside look like?

I have my book to read which I am enjoying, it adds another layer when you read it again and you know how it ends.

On the journey, I eat my persimmon. It feels strange biting into something that looks so much like an orange. I am new to these, my daughter, Ciara, showed them to me in November.

It turns out persimmons are quite difficult to eat on a bus. I need a wet wipe now and I don't have any. When I'm finished, I am still not sure what I ate, it's such a new flavour and I am not sure why I haven't eaten one before. It's like if an apple and a melon had a baby. It also turns out that big, flat pastry things you buy in a Málaga bakery at 9.00 pm. in the evening are not good bus food either. The pastry is difficult to snap and very sticky.

Out of the window, clusters of villages decorate the distant hills as we keep moving, all painted white with brown roofs. The countryside has more gentle inclines and mountains further away. It reminds me of the Meseta, the vast countryside on my Camino, all beige and green with neat rows of olive trees.

The roads weave in and out at the base of the hills, cutting through valleys. We come to a hair pin bend and I see more gorgeous villages clustered together tightly.

At Ardales, a gorgeous town up a steep road that wasn't made for buses, we stop to let two girls off and go back down the hill, some of it in reverse. The scenery is breath-taking. Some fields have been cultivated, looking like bright gold sand dunes framed by distant mountains.

But I am not good on buses and there's lots of swinging left and right. So, by now, I am feeling a bit sick. Then, in the middle of nowhere, we drop another seven people off – two different families who get into cars waiting for them. They must live in one of those rural villages. Now it's six kilometres till Ronda. I have been looking forward to this for months and very excited that this will be my first proper stop on this trip.

I stare out of the window as we arrive, taking it all in. It's busy, with long straight roads. The buildings have iron looking balconies which gives it an historic feel.

I find my way easily from the bus station to my hotel, Hotel Sevilla, and it's very nice, considering it wasn't too much money. The room might be bland with a view of a brick wall but that's OK. It's big, spotless, comfortable and it has a bath. I am not going to be spending much time in the room as I will be out exploring, so the view out of the window doesn't matter.

I don't waste any time, heading straight out for a stroll to get my bearings.

It's a short walk to the town and on the right are some gardens, so I cross the road to take a look, discovering they're spacious and tidy with neat flower beds. As the gardens come to an end, the vista opens up. There is a large floor area, a row of pillars, and a stunning view of the mountains. It's quite breath-taking.

I walk towards the railings and find I am on the edge of a cliff with a dramatic drop straight down.

Wow.

This is the reason that I came to Ronda but I wasn't expecting to see it so soon. I am totally blown away by the scale of it. The photos were so impressive online that you sometimes wonder if it's just clever photography but being here is something else entirely.

I can't believe I am standing on the edge of a gorge and protected from falling down a huge, sheer drop by ornate metal railings. You can still see through them down to the green floor of the valley.

To my left, the flat edge of the gorge juts out and it reminds me of a giant slice of Victoria sponge with the buildings sat on the top like icing. It's as straight as if it were cut with a knife. Absolutely spectacular.

I can't believe I am here enjoying it. This is such a treat.

Waves of emotion suddenly hit me. Travel always does this. I think it's because I feel blessed to be in this stunning place, experiencing it. Also because it's a solo trip. I picked this place from hundreds that I could have visited in the world, and I found my way here all by myself.

It's so different to Málaga which I loved but for different reasons. Life really is for living and I am doing my best to enjoy it.

It's very peaceful here but I can just hear some music, probably coming from the old town to my left. It sounds like an accordion.

I stand here and take it all in for a moment. It's a bit of a shock getting off a bus and so soon arrive somewhere so dramatic.

It makes me wonder how many beautiful places there are in the world, and how can I get to see them all?

I am so grateful that I had the courage to book this trip. It's not courageous travelling, as such, although I know from the many conversations I have had, that many people disagree. I think the courage is finding the time, prioritising yourself above everything else going on in your life, and actually booking the plane, boat or train ticket. That's the bit that often doesn't get done because we throw obstacles in the way. Once you have committed to booking something, you generally go.

That song by Avicii where he says he wants to travel the world, but doesn't have any plans, always touches me. You have to put your wishes into action. Find the time, find the money and book your tickets, and you end up in places like this, standing on the edge of a gorge pinching yourself.

I walk towards the old town and hopefully to the famous bridge which crosses the gorge, wandering through more gardens until I see an ornate band stand with the same view across the vast countryside. There, a man plays beautiful music on an accordion which melts my heart. I drop some coins in his case and sit down to listen and look at this view. Both complement each other so well.

I love an accordion, my grandad had one but I don't have many memories of him playing it. I was only ten years old when he died and we didn't see a great deal of him. I have always wanted to play one. On a night out on Lady Daphne, a Thames sailing barge now docked in Charlestown Harbour in Cornwall, a lady played a similar instrument and, as soon as I got home that night, I researched how much they were and how to play them because it touched me so much. One day, I think I am going to buy one, although I am not that musical. I was pretty good at the recorder at school, as many children my age were, and I remember it giving me a lot of comfort. I remember that it cheered me up when I was feeling low and I got to play it in school assemblies, which for a shy little girl was quite an achievement. So, I can at least read music at a very basic level. It's such a wonderful noise, this accordion, an old fashioned, happy noise.

From this spot, I even get a good view of the impressive bridge that straddles the gorge. Ronda has already exceeded my expectations and I haven't been here an hour yet.

I drag myself away and pop into the tourist information hub which is just a short walk near the bull ring – I have no intention of going in there. I accidentally got involved with bulls and Spanish culture on my Camino, in a beautiful little town called Viana. I can still remember the smell of them and their solid heavy bodies. I had mixed feelings then about bulls and Spanish culture but it has all been accidental. But I won't be going into the bull ring on this trip.

A very helpful lady gives me lots of bits of paper. I thought I would chill here in Ronda before I go to Seville, but it looks like there's plenty to do if I wanted to.

Leaving the tourist information hub, I go for a stroll and walk across the bridge with its stunning views on both sides, then head through the old town alongside an old fort wall with weathered terracotta-coloured bricks. I capture a stunning photo of this ancient wall, the white houses in the distance, such beautiful colours.

I continue down this old cobblestoned path, wanting to know more about its history the further I go. The cobbles must be authentic; they are all different shapes and very uneven.

After so much exploring, I am feeling hungry now and need to find a hot meal of some sort. I haven't eaten since Sunday evening.

I see a little Spanish café down a street between the shops, just a slim little café with one row of tables lined against the wall, but I can't read the menu and so walk past. It's only €10 for a meal of the day. As I am walking away, I give myself a stern talking to and go back. I am not going to find better than that.

They don't speak English here but we figure it out with my little bit of Spanish. I order lentils for the first course and something with potatoes for the second. Bread and a drink is included so I choose an orange Kas, which reminds me of my Camino.

The café is very Spanish, with a bar area hosting three men sat on stools, who look like work men, chatting and laughing. People walk past the front of the café and wave to the staff. One of the staff even gives a rather sad, tatty looking man a free coffee with a smile and a tap on the arm. I like it here.

The lentil soup is delicious, and I decide I must use these little round lentils more in cooking. With some surprise, I realise that the word I didn't recognise on the menu is pork. Oh well, I'm starving.

It's starting to drizzle a bit now, so I pay the bill and say thank you very much. As they are just closing, I am grateful that they fed me, and I step out into the rain, stopping in a tiny corner shop to pick up some biscuits.

When I get back to the hotel, I need hot water from the coffee machine downstairs in the lounge area so I put some loose green tea in the bottom of my flask and go and get it filled up, and then rest in my room for a bit.

Later, after it's dark, I go out again to see the Christmas lights. I need my hat and gloves as it's a little chilly, and find it's pretty relaxed here compared to last night in Málaga. Ronda has ordinary Christmas lights similar to what you see in any town in England, especially the ones hanging over the roads.

It all feels quite normal except that there's no real tree, just a lit-up cone-shaped one similar to Málaga, pretending to be a tree. This one changes colour every few minutes which makes it even less Christmassy. It seems a little false and not homely like a fir tree.

Despite the time of year, I am still not feeling Christmassy. I like the lights but they are not making me homesick for Christmas. I wondered how I would feel experiencing Christmas somewhere else but it's not affecting me much. The lights in Málaga didn't either and they were phenomenal. I loved the extravagance of them, all the people and the Spanish songs, but it still didn't bring me any Christmas feelings.

It's cold but some pretty Spanish streets have restaurant tables outside which surprises me. I would need to keep my gloves on if I were eating outside this evening, it is December. I see somewhere that I might have breakfast tomorrow and walk back to my room. It's been quite a day and I have walked 15,879 steps.

I really want a lovely soak in the bath tonight but there's no plug. Well, that's not going to stop me. I put my flannel in a plastic bag and wedge it where the plug should be. The tub fills up and I enjoy my bath, ready for bed.

Thursday 21st December

Today is the shortest day of the year which always feels like an important date on the calendar. The nights will slowly start pulling out now and we are halfway through the winter. I like the idea of travelling in the winter, especially somewhere warmer than England. The long English winter will hopefully feel a bit shorter when I return home. I might do this again, I might do it every year.

For now though, I am going to try a walking tour around Ronda and learn some of its history. The lady in the tourist information hub yesterday told me to ring at 9.30 am. but I don't like using my phone, so I will walk down to speak to her in person, it's only ten minutes.

On the way, I go to 'the edge' again to admire the view with the low sunlight of the morning. It feels even more impressive at this time. It's really cold though, with a real nip in the air.

I am told there might be a walking tour at 4.00 pm. but they need three more people for it to go ahead. So it's not looking promising.

Instead, I buy the ticket that will get me into a few attractions. There's a choice of paying €25 or €12. I go for the cheaper one, mainly because I don't want to wear myself out. Plus, it includes a visit to the bridge, where I think you can go inside, which is the only thing I really want to do here. When I saw a photo of Ronda, I just wanted to get here. I could obviously see the bridge in photos and I have walked over it but I had no idea that you could go in it, or that this town was so full of history and places to visit.

Then the lady behind the counter charges me €9.00.

I am insulted. She has charged me the retired person's price. It's the first time this has happened to me and I am not an OAP, although I obviously look like one. After recoiling from the shock of it, I walk away laughing. It's very sad to look older than you are and she didn't even ask so she absolutely thought I looked retired. Fat chance, I won't get my pension for another nine years.

This is the new phase of life I am moving into, like when you are a teenager and have to start paying full fares on a bus but try to get away with not paying it for ages. I once got a child's fare on a train going to Felixstowe from Ipswich when I was 24, and I didn't ask for it. I was so shocked that I didn't correct him. My youthful looks don't seem to be working the other end of my life.

I knew when I stopped dying my hair that it would age me and it definitely has but that's the decision that I made. The bonus is that I don't have to buy hair dye which saves me money and I don't have to dye it every month or so, which saves me time and stress. The downside is I look old.

But do I care? If I'm honest, only a tiny bit and the bonus is that I saved €3.00. Before this happened, I had already made up my mind to treat myself to breakfast in a local café and now I have three euros to spend towards it.

The café I choose is lovely inside with a stunning mural on the wall. It's full of Spanish people and Enola Gay by OMD is playing on the radio which is a bit random. They find the most unusual songs to play in Spain, ones that I have forgotten all about.

I talk in Spanish to a staff member, ordering a veggie breakfast, and feel very proud of myself. I soon find out, too, that the veggie breakfast is delicious. Then off I go to visit the six attractions on my OAP ticket.

Firstly, I am going to the bridge, Puente Nuevo, which means new bridge. I am going into it which seems an unusual thing to do. To reach it, I walk down some steps until I am under one of the arches, which feels like being under a viaduct with a huge piece of arched stone above my head.

Before me, there are railings and a huge drop into the actual gorge. I am now spanning the deep crevice of the gorge, it's quite something. To get inside, I climb up a few old steps in a narrow passageway and arrive in what feels like a room with a tall ceiling but it's the centre of the bridge. There's no one here, just me. I can now go to the window and look out across the gorge and the countryside.

Inside, there are some screens on the wall, showing how it was built. They are fascinating, this is such an interesting structure with lots of history.

There are also photos of the gorge without the bridge and photos of the construction, completed in 1789. It's 120 metres to the bottom. Apparently, this room has been used as a prison, a torture chamber, and it's possible some people have been thrown out of the window, or even jumped.

This was the second bridge; the first bridge completely collapsed in 1741 and killed 50 people, which must have been devastating for the town. For the bridge to collapse is awful when they were trying so hard to build such an unusual structure, but to lose that many people in one event must have been tough.

A glass panel sits where one of the floor tiles has been removed and, through it, there's a tiny hole where you can see right down to the grass at the bottom of the gorge. Right at this moment, there is nothing underneath me, and cars driving over my head.

However, I'm finding it all very enjoyable and take it all in before I go back down the stairs to get out.

Just next to the bridge, I go to the Palacio de Congresos de Ronda. It's not that interesting, although it is a very old house and has a large courtyard and arches but I don't stay very long.

The sun has come out now it's warming up and there's not a cloud in the sky. I continue exploring with more cobblestones underfoot, down steep slopes in the old town, until I reach a great viewpoint. To the left are those white houses with the brown roofs, the countryside, mountains, and green fields. I can hear birds singing and sheep in the fields far away with their bells.

The next stop on my ticket is Ronda's Arab baths, Baños Árabes. These baths were built here for the Muslims who washed before prayer. The plaque says the baths were for meeting places as well.

Everything, again, is very old and almost in ruins.

It looks quite strange as you enter. It's all outdoors and in front of me is a roof to a building that I can't see. The building must be sunken into the ground because I am higher than the roof right now. There are lots of round windows on it which are raised. I can't quite work out what that is. But I go down some really old steps and enter the underground baths.

Everything seems to be made of rough, old stone. The first room is a long thin room with a rounded roof and star-shaped holes from it that let in the light. There is a stone bath at one end and I can almost picture the water in it. There are two more separate rooms as I explore further, of similar sizes, with the roofs letting in light again. I would love a TARDIS to go back in time, although I suspect it will be full of naked or half-dressed men. But I would love to see the baths in use, feel the temperature, and hear the conversations. In the last room, there's a film show and a few chairs in rows before it but it's in Spanish so I go outside for a wander.

It's a beautiful day and so peaceful here on the edge of the town.

I go up a steep little slope of uneven cobbles and see that there is a waterwheel at the top before wandering back down. When I go back inside, the English film is starting.

It's chilly underground in the stone rooms but the photos on the film are very atmospheric. It brings this site alive with clever images of how it used to be, how the people looked, and how these baths were used.

Apparently, they were built between the 13th and 15th century. I enjoyed a trip to the Roman baths in Bath, England once and went in. I even put my hands in the water. This feels different because the walls are rough stone and there isn't any water. You have to imagine it and the film really brings it to life. It's also much smaller. These baths are near the stream just outside the town. The water was obviously needed to make the baths work.

The three rooms here, although they are just pillars and stone now, would have been three different temperatures. The hottest room was nearest to the water supply and heated with a furnace. The hot water was directed underground. The other two rooms were not as hot. The video shows lots of benches where the men would sit and chat to each other. It's a very interesting presentation.

I walk straight back up the slope I visited moments before as now I know it's where the donkey walked up to the waterwheel so that he could walk around to move the wheel. It all makes sense now after the film and I can feel the history so much better. It was just a slope before but now I can see the cobbles where the donkey walked and the aqueduct that took the water down to the baths.

This has been a treat, I've loved it.

As I seem to have walked a long way down to the baths and the sun is shining, I do the walk that I was saving till tomorrow, which is to get to the bottom of the gorge and look back up at the bridge.

Unfortunately, I must go up before going back down, so it's a tough walk as it's getting warmer. But soon I have to stop – it's too much and I am baking. I sit on a wall with a great view of the countryside and white houses, and take my raincoat and scarf off to drink tea from my flask. It's good to have a little rest.

I feel so lucky to be here. Ronda is such an amazing place.

Thinking back, I was so anxious before I left, worrying about everything but now I am not worrying.

I am in the moment which happens when you travel, exploring and looking, listening, reading and lapping it all up. I have travelled a little bit now in my life, so I do know that this happens but it's still a surprise, how life's worries can just melt away and become less significant than they are when you are at home.

This is such a good spot for a cuppa. I like bringing a flask because you can find lovely spots without looking for a café and queuing up, and it's instant.

Speaking of worries though, and one that won't go away, is that my son, Liam, will be driving home today for six or seven hours. But I have said out loud a few times, 'Safe travels,' as if passing on the responsibility to the universe to look after him so that I can have a day off from worrying. Hopefully it works.

Now, I put my sunglasses on and get my selfie stick out

and try to capture this moment, then follow the map through the old high fort wall into a charming piazza with people chilling in the sunshine.

I find the way down to the cobbled road and walk through the old town, the path leading out into the countryside.

It's spectacular at the bottom of the gorge. I look up and see the bandstand I was sitting on yesterday, it's so tiny, like a little old fashioned bird cage. The bridge is just as impressive from down here and high above me is the little window that I was looking out of just a few hours ago.

I sit on a rock and take it all in, this place is so awe-inspiring. I open my flask and finish my tea. The bridge is quite a technical feat connecting the two sides of the gorge, it's not surprising there's a history of tragedy attached to it. It's very striking from any angle, I am glad that I went into it first and learnt about how it was built before coming down here.

As I'm sitting on my rock, a German lady passes who has just been to Brazil and she speaks English fluently, so I tell her about the walking tour at four o'clock. She understands I am trying to fill the spots so it goes ahead and thinks it's funny.

After a while, I stop staring at the bridge and the amazing gorge to struggle back up the steep winding road, having to stop quite a few times. I go back to the plaza and sit down on a wall to find my map.

I need to eat something, it's been five hours since breakfast. So, I choose an outdoor cafe with lots of seating spaced out across a big area that I considered eating at yesterday, some tables shaded under trees and palms. It was €13 to eat here yesterday and it's €10 today. I find a spot and order the set menu and a Fanta orange.

The soup is delicious but the second course comes out before I have finished the first, and the chips are so cold and greasy I can't eat them. The staff here also haven't brought me any cutlery. I tried to get the man's attention but because of the layout of the garden and where I chose to sit, he hasn't come by. Or maybe he just doesn't care. Defeated, I plonk the sausage in the soup and eat it with my spoon.

Even though the food isn't that great, there is some upbeat

music, palm trees and blue skies surrounding me and it's a treat to eat outdoors in December. I have spoken Spanish here as well.

I order a flan for dessert which is included, but it's not a flan, it's a brown wobbly thing with a big pile of cream which I don't like. I thought it would be pastry.

I can't complain really, and I'm not going to, but it's only just worth €10, if that. To be honest, it's good value, just about, but I wouldn't return.

With my meal finished, I am now going to the last building on my list. Casa del Gigante. I have no idea what it is.

After this, I will have done the bulk of Ronda. There are many more buildings that I could go in but I won't.

Casa del Gigante is an interesting building, a small palace with some lovely features that I manage to see in five minutes. But there is a lovely video similar to the one in the baths, showing the development of civilization from 5,000 years ago with some stunning images of Ronda which is fascinating.

Following this, I explore the last building over the courtyard but find it's an art museum which only takes three minutes to view.

As I walk past a large church again – very tall and dominant with huge high walls – I am curious about going inside. It is huge, and surrounded by houses, with a path all the way around and it seems to have only one entrance. I find the door, discovering this church is called Iglesia de Santa María la Mayor, and it's €4.50 to get in, on top of the money I paid for my multi-ticket. I pay it.

Inside, it's a proper Spanish bling church like the ones on my Camino, home to a big gold altar, with beautiful murals on the walls and a white ceiling. There is also a lot of stone, and chunky pillars and arches. I find the way up to the roof terrace up some scary stone stairs. This was the reason that I paid to come in, I like a roof terrace.

The roof is really surprising; there's a wide wooden platform built right onto it. It feels very safe and secure but quite unusual and it wraps around a couple sides of the church, giving me even more views of Ronda. This time though, more residential as we are surrounded by white houses. The brown roofs are made of the same half-cylindrical tiles of slightly different colours, so they look mismatched but give a great rustic feel.

It's so peaceful in the direct sunlight.

From here, up a few steps is a tiny door which reads 'Open' in four languages, so I open it and go in. Wow, I am now inside the church, really high up, on a little balcony that's just a few feet wide. I am level with the top of the huge stone column and I can see all the way to the bottom. I can't believe this. No one is here, just me, up high, enjoying looking down. I take loads of photos and come out smiling. I explore the walkway skirting the outer edge of the church again and sit on a bench in the sunshine. It's really peaceful, being so high up, and the view of the town is wonderful. I can hear the accordion playing lovely music again. It's a good job it's enjoyable as it reaches right over Ronda.

So here I am, sitting high on a walkway on the outside of a church with views of mountains and white painted houses in front of me, with the sun warming my face and a man somewhere out there playing lovely music. Does life get any better?

I just sit and take it all in for a while. It's 4.30 pm. What a full day I have had.

Another 15 minutes passes by while I just chill, listening and watching the birds, until I eventually make my way down the stone spiral stairs and into the main church. Looking back up at where I was, which is such a long way, I realise I have been up very high and down very low in the last 24 hours. What a funny old day.

On my way back, I see a gift shop and want to buy something but I only have €10 left in cash. I really need to pluck up the courage to get some more money out but I am so nervous over the possibility that I won't see my card again.

Nonetheless, I do see a machine attached to a Carrefour – a zap one, which is great as it won't eat my card, but I can barely read all the instructions. Once I've figured it out, I request to take €200 out and see it's a bad exchange rate, plus a fee of €3.95. I decide to just do it as I can't bear the stress, but I must accidentally press cancel instead as it shuts down. Do I wait? Did I cancel the transaction?

I put my Wi-Fi on to look at my Monzo app and no transaction appears, just the one from the church an hour ago. I wait a few minutes in case it is delayed coming through.

Nothing. Phew. I walk on and find another machine inside a bank which feels safer. I think next time I might bring a credit card when travelling, or any other card in case a machine does eat it, which it probably won't but it saves me some worry.

This cash machine gives me English options to read and the figures are better. It all goes through and my card comes back, phew, that was scary.

I walk 'home' via the edge of the gorge with the huge drop just so that I can look again. On the way, I find a corner shop with lots of fruit so I get another persimmon and two bananas for breakfast, and a bag of cherry chocolate sweets and a can of cider I have never seen before. I also pass a posh bakery and pop in to buy four miniature pastry cakes for €1.80.

I go back to my room, empty my flask, refill with fresh tea leaves and go downstairs for some hot water.

What a day. My app says I've walked 22,722 steps, no wonder I ache. It's now 6.10 pm. and time to chill.

I scroll through my photos while drinking tea and eating the most amazing chocolate that cost only €1.20. I will be popping back to get more of those. The cake things are weird, a little stale and greasy, and just weird, but the tea is perfect.

Next I drink the cider and finish off the crisps that I got in Málaga.

Thinking ahead, I have booked a bus for Saturday from here to Seville. I'm so excited to get there. When I got this mad idea to go away for Christmas, Seville was the first place that I thought of. It seems such a long time ago now when I made that decision that I can't remember why I even picked it. I just hope it's lovely as that's where I will be spending Christmas Day.

But I am not in a hurry to leave Ronda, I have really

enjoyed this town and there's lots more that I could have done. I am also really excited about my day trip tomorrow to Setenil.

I read my book set in Córdoba for a little while and go to sleep.

Friday 22nd December

Well, a belly full of weird little cakes, some crisps and too many cherry chocolates, all washed down with a flask of tea and a small can of Spanish cider, hasn't given me the best night's sleep.

I woke up at about 3.00 am. with a nightmare, and a few more times besides. I am glad to be awake now and know that it was only that – a nightmare. I haven't had one in six months; my subconscious must be mulling something over and I wish it wouldn't.

Gosh, it's cold outside. At 7.45 am., it's still dark and I'm standing in the street near the bus stop. A sign nearby says it's five degrees and I am grateful for my woolly hat. There's nowhere here to buy a ticket, just a café that sounds busy even before you see it, buzzing with men propping the counter up and chatting which is lovely to see.

I sit on a metal bench outside but the metal is freezing so I get up and stroll about. Hopefully I can buy a ticket on the bus. I have some loose change, a €5 note and my card; one of those should buy me a ticket to Setenil.

When the bus arrives, I'm relieved that it's only €2.20 for one way, and I pay with cash. As we leave Ronda, the early sun lights up the mountains. It's only a short journey, less than half an hour, I think.

I am very excited to get there. I have seen some amazing photos of Setenil on the internet. Whenever I am researching a place to visit, I join Facebook pages relating to the place, and on one of the Seville pages there were photos of Setenil de las Bodegas, which I really liked the look of. When I saw how close it was to Ronda, it made perfect sense to visit.

We ride along the dual carriageway then come off it and stop in a cute village full of white houses which is very busy with families and children. People are sitting on tables outside restaurants with their coats on.

Three chatty women hop on the bus and one talks to me

and laughs. I have no idea what she has said, so I just smile. They all talk too fast and with different accents to what I'm used to on Duolingo.

There's another village up ahead, with houses so white that it's blinding, like the White Cliffs of Dover, only much smaller. I bet it's nice there, wherever it is.

Soon enough, we pull into Setenil bus station and I walk a little way and then turn a corner – and oh my.

I feel like I have walked onto a film set, this doesn't look real.

It's difficult to describe because I've never seen anything like it before. There's a huge overhanging rock jutting out, leaving a space underneath where there are more white buildings, looking like they are tucked right into the rock. Their roofs are the rock, and you can only see the front of the buildings.

It looks like there is a river meandering and a thick concrete wall to stop you from falling in. Between the wall and the front of the buildings and cafés, there is a wide path to walk on, actually under the huge rock overhang. It has created a kind of tunnel effect. There is a big, green dangling plant hanging off the rock too, and into the river. It's dramatic, unusual, and beautiful all at the same time.

I am so glad I came to visit.

Frost covers the parked cars in front of the cafés and under the rock. There's no one around. Some cafés are still just opening up, and it's very quiet here at 9.30 am.

Further ahead, a bridge stands over the water and near it is a signpost with a map entices me to take a look. Over the little bridge, the area is just as impressive. The street is narrower on this side and, here, the rock looks almost volcanic, as if it was once fluid and slipped down the mountain. There are buildings underneath, which look like they are in the rock too, causing huge shadows. Houses are lined on both sides with the rock crawling across the top, creating the feel of a tunnel.

It's stunning.

I take my time wandering around this unique village with its white painted houses. It gets slightly less dramatic as you leave the centre and more residential, but the houses are still in the rock.

Over the river where it meanders away, a condensed area of white houses sits on a hill with steep lanes. Some are not near the rock, so they look like the houses of a typical white Spanish village but as you get closer to where I was standing before, the houses are once more sheltered by this beautiful feature.

At the top of some steps, I find myself in a spot where the word Setenil is spelt out in individual letters a few feet high, where you can take your photo, proving that you were here, so I pose and take one next to the sign. From here, I can see what looks like a huge church perched right at the top of the hill, before I go back down, then back up because it's not making much sense, though it's lovely to walk around.

A narrow set of steps lead up another gorgeous steep street. The pretty path with shallow steps is the same colour as the rock hanging over the top of the white buildings, and I can just see glimpses of blue sky. It's gorgeous.

A plaque on the wall says I am in Calle Herrería Setenil de las Bodegas. It also says that it is:

'One of the most beautiful and romantic Andalusia streets. With its 'Besamé en este rincón' (Kiss me in the corner), it represents one of the most special streets in the urban landscape of Setenil. La Herreria, defined by some authors as 'one of the most beautiful Andalusian streets', is a street lined with cave houses, stepped and narrow, that leads down to the river. Walking along this street between limestone facades and geraniums will take us into a surreal world halfway between mineral chemistry and romantic literature.'

Just as I am pondering those words on the plaque, I see the cutest little café, just by the 'Kiss me in the corner'. The little twist in the street provides a little area where the café sits. It has an outdoor seating area with one table where I am going to sit and take a break.

It's 10.30 am. now and definitely time to stop. This seems

the perfect place. Sometimes I can make my mind up really quickly.

Luckily, there is a railing in the outdoor seating area to stop you falling onto the street below. It's a beautiful spot, surrounded by these pretty white houses. The view up the narrow street is gorgeous, as well as the one where I just walked under the rock face. This café is a cave house like the others, with just the white front, a big wooden door, and poinsettia flowers everywhere which look amazing against the painted walls.

I go inside to look at the menu and see that I am now inside the cave, the back of it being a wonky wall, which slants forward over the serving area and till. Anyone tall would have to watch they didn't bang their head.

I order a gazpacho and a green tea then sit outside. The sun is warming up, the sky is bright blue, and I am in a beautiful spot. It's amazing, again.

The gazpacho is delicious, a strange but perfect breakfast. The lady takes a photo of me as I want to capture this moment and I know that this is going to be one of my favourites. It might get as far as a frame.

With breakfast over, I decide to keep climbing up to the castle only to find that the tourist information is not open. I ask a man what time it will be open in Spanish, and he just says later.

After wandering around Setenil some more, I find myself back on the first street that I arrived in, so stop in another café under the rock and order a second breakfast. Toast and tomato, and the tiniest cup of tea. The toast is amazing – a warm roll with a pot of tomatoes at its side to spread on it.

I love it here in this unique village and want to lap it all up. I order another cup of tea and ask for a bigger cup. It's still small, just not tiny. As I relax, I write up my journal but it's difficult not to be distracted by the huge overhanging rock.

There is a bus at 12.30 pm. but I decide to get the 2.30 pm. one instead and go for a walk as I will probably not return here. Not because it isn't lovely but because it's a bit out of the way. Plus, I am heading for 60 in a big hurry so there's limited time left to travel and far too many new places to explore. I would highly recommend Setenil to anyone who is in the area.

Before I leave, I am going to go inside this strange cave building to compare it to the other café. The toilet is a standalone room in the corner because there are no straight walls; the stone walls and ceiling simply blend into one so there's no corners. It's very dramatic.

The bill for both teas and the toast is only €3.20. Funny, as I thought I would pay premium prices here but it's extremely cheap. Then, off I go for another stroll in the sunshine.

The streets are busy now with cars, vans, and people. I go past the same little piazza I have walked past before and cars and vans are parked everywhere now delivering to the restaurants. It's so pretty, with lots of flowers and orange trees.

I reach the tourist information again although it's not very exciting. The lady here doesn't speak any English which is good because I have to practise again. It's much less daunting when they can't speak English, they are grateful that you can communicate anything at all to help the situation.

A board outside says it's €2.00 to go to Museo de la Casa de la Damita, so I buy a ticket and the lady explains where it is but, after much exploring, I still can't find it. I ask a tiny Spanish lady instead, much shorter than me (which is rare), who points me in the right direction.

The Museo de la Casa de la Damita is a room upstairs with 12 very old photos of people who lived here many years ago. It doesn't take me very long to see it all so I go back to the tourist information lady who sends me over the road and points to stairs, saying, 'Arriba.'

Once I'm there, I see artwork in a room that takes only 10 seconds to look at but more stairs lead upwards so up I go. They are steep, taking me to an empty room with a lookout but the tiny window is dirty and I can't see anything. More steps go higher and I come out onto the roof. I am not sure I should be here, but I am and there's no one to ask, or stop me. I wander around and look at the views on all sides, it's quite impressive.

I can see the village from here that we passed earlier on the bus, way in the distance. It's a lovely viewpoint, making everything look very condensed at this angle. I go back down, discovering my legs are like jelly now from all that climbing.

Back at the first overhang where I had my toast, all the seats are now taken in all the restaurants, with lots of people chatting and chairs scraping. Such a contrast to the frost and woolly hat weather this morning. I am lucky to have experienced both. I got great photos earlier when no one was around.

On the way back to the bus station, I stop at a little stall and buy a cork passport cover, hoping it fits, and a cork card holder for Ciara. I have spent a few pennies in this place but it's been fun. It's really warm as I sit by the bus stop and wait, and I have to take my hoodie off.

Setenil is a wow place, a one-hundred-photographs kind of place. Charming, pretty, charismatic, honest, real, rustic and gorgeous. I am so glad that I visited.

When the bus driver arrives, it seems like he knows everyone. He drives with his arm out of the window and shouts greetings, and chats to the passengers while driving. Setenil is a small place and I don't know if people here stay here for generations or move about. He might have been a bus driver all his life in this area.

Back at the hotel, I make a cup of tea and rest for a bit as I walked 15,000 steps in Setenil.

It's 3.45 pm. and, whilst I am tired, I need to go out and enjoy the last bit of sunshine, maybe look for food.

I take a slow stroll around town. Lots of people are out enjoying the glorious weather. The accordion man is playing again too, so I sit on the band stand and listen.

Next, I make my way to the café which has a great view of the gorge. I don't mind if I eat something here or just get a drink. When I ask for just a drink, the waiter suggests I sit in the shade so when he walks off, I look at a menu on one of the tables and decide to have soup, if I can sit in the sun by the dramatic gorge and bridge.

This is where I wanted to sit and I don't care what I do

while I am here. I have an uninterrupted view of the gorge, with its ragged edges and I can see right down to the bottom. I first fell in love with gorges as a child when, as a family, we went to Cheddar in Somerset. I can still remember staring out of the car window, craning my neck to see the huge cliffs on either side. I have been back as an adult a couple of times and it still feels just as dramatic. This gorge is too uneven to have a road on the bottom and it winds much more.

This is another close view of the bridge which makes me happy, and where I can see the stunning countryside through the arches.

I order a cold garlic soup, Sopa de Ajo blanco, and a glass of sangria, a bit spontaneous and another strange combination.

The soup is harsh though. I had this with my friend, Emma, when we were walking the Camino in a vegan restaurant in Burgos and it was delicious, but this version isn't. It gets harsher and harsher and the stale bread roll isn't helping.

This place has linen tablecloths and waiters so I thought the food would be better. But at least it's worth coming here for a view of the gorge. I can see the other small bridge as well by the baths, with people on it. I have got a feel for this place now, despite its odd geographical layout. It's all about the gorge here and everything works around it.

I am going to miss Ronda. It's been much more than I imagined it would be, and I love nature when it shines like this and there is so much history here.

I can't finish this soup however, it's too garlicky, strong, and very bitter. I have run out of bread too, and can't possibly eat it on its own.

Ahead of me, the sun is just dipping down behind the bridge and there is a chill in the air now, so it's time to go. I was lucky to get here and enjoy this spot in the sunshine while I could. I slowly finish my sangria, get the bill and see they have charged me €1.00 for the stale roll. Hmm.

I start my walk back to my hotel and take a right up the shopping street. I fancy a Christmas souvenir but haven't found anything yet. One shop has some real tat with the lettering falling off, so I don't want that. I wonder what Spanish people's homes look like, are they decorated? If so, where do they buy their Christmas decorations from because I can't find anything? I want a door hanger like the one in the café in Setenil.

Apart from the lights hanging up, there is very little Christmas anywhere. The odd token window sticker but absolutely nothing like at home.

It's a bit strange. I knew it would be different here and I was looking forward to seeing those differences but, so far, there isn't very much seasonal décor or feeling, so I can't compare.

I haven't felt Christmassy at all yet, which is OK, but it simply doesn't feel like it will be Christmas in three days.

My partner, Phil, messaged earlier to say he was going out to buy new tree lights. This is what I was hoping to escape, the commitment to Christmas that we have in England. As if Christmas wouldn't be Christmas without a fully functioning set of lights or all the other things that we think are important. The expectations are high for everything to be in place. We set it all up, get everything right and then we are too tired and stressed to enjoy it. Not one person would say, 'That's OK, we don't have to replace the lights,' because it's all these things and structures that make Christmas what it is and we have to obey it. So far in Spain, I haven't seen that enthusiasm that we have in England.

Perhaps when I get to Seville tomorrow it will be different. Or maybe not.

I make my way back to the hotel, having bought nothing, and quite tired as I have walked 25,376 steps today.

I hope Seville is lovely and maybe I can talk to some more people there. It's not been lonely here, I do enjoy my own company, but I would like to interact a bit more.

Especially with it being Christmas.

Saturday 23rd December

I slept really well last night, even though my rumbling tummy was trying to stop me, and I am still hungry but I have a two and a half hour bus ride so I can't eat anything or I might be sick. When I get to Seville, I need to find some proper food, full of vitamins, nutrition and flavour. The bus will reach Seville at 1.50 pm., and with a 23-minute walk to my hotel, I completely forgot that I booked a walking tour for 5.00 pm. I am glad they emailed to remind me. So I will eat as soon as I arrive in Seville with my case, rather than find my hotel and then go out to eat.

People have often said to me that I am brave to travel alone. I don't consider it brave, but I do understand why people say that. We are all different, which is a good thing, but I do worry about really silly things that probably don't bother other people. I don't do this without a level of anxiety.

Right now, I am at the bus station sitting on the coldest metal bench ever made and cover my suitcase with my bright blue rain cover from TK Maxx.

Why? So it's visible, and ugly, and hopefully won't be pinched. It's way too big and has holes in it from dragging it to the airport in Bristol. The fact it's unattractive is good. It's like putting a baby grow on a baby and doing the poppers up underneath. This fetching bright blue cover's purpose is for its journey in the bus hold. I will spot it if someone tries to steal it and, whilst this would seem very over-the-top to some people, it makes me feel more in control. When you travel alone, something is always going to worry you. For some, it would be the languages, or getting to accommodation, or eating alone. I am OK with all of those. My fear is losing my belongings.

I really don't enjoy this bit, waiting for a bus. It's 11.25 am. The bus is not here yet and it's due at 11.30 am. There are three in the bus lanes ahead and one says Torremolinos but under it, Seville, which doesn't make sense as they are in opposite directions.

But my bus is still not here after waiting a little bit more and so I go and investigate. It's chaos at the Torremolinos bus. Everyone is huddled around waving their phones at the poor driver. It doesn't look like all these people will fit.

I ask the lady next to me if this bus is going to Seville and she said it is, and to ask the driver as it's not a Damas bus that I was looking for.

For some reason, he looks at my phone over the crowds, hones in on the screen and says yes, meaning I get to struggle through the people for the door. I was going to put my bag in the hold but I'm scared if I don't get on the bus right now that I might lose my spot. There's not much room for my feet but I am OK.

Finally, I sit back and the driver starts counting the seats. He lets more people on, then returns behind the wheel. A man gets on and asks in English for two tickets to Seville. Phew. I am definitely on the right bus.

I can smell stale alcohol from someone who had too much to drink last night. This might be a difficult journey, especially if I throw up.

The bus leaves the station, and I think I need a wee already.

As we drive along, the scenery out of the window is full of tall, imposing craggy mountains that, sometimes, the bus weaves through, sometimes it's further away. Gradually, the view settles down to low gentle hills the colour of the Meseta, a soft green and hay colour with a sprinkling of painted white villages.

I hate buses, especially when they are packed, and my suitcase is where my feet should be. I am trying very hard not to look at the time and, when I do, it's not moving much.

Oh dear, I'm starting to feel a little sick, I need a wee and I'm a bit trapped. A man behind me is snoring. I might get a train next time. For now, I read my Kindle which makes the time go quicker.

Then Seville comes into view, it's huge, the buildings on the horizon stretching for miles. The normal outskirts of a city. Then we go over the river and everyone starts shuffling about.

We have 20 minutes to go, but it looks like we are here. How exciting.

Once we all get off the bus, I google where I can get vegan food and almost run there as I am so hungry, my bag making a racket along the floor tiles, at last reaching a stall in a market. The stalls here are permanent with proper shop fronts which you don't go in. Instead, a row of seating is placed in the middle between the stalls.

I find the loo and then go back and order, in Spanish. People are starting to talk back to me, I can't really understand the words but with hand gestures and the context it makes sense. I order a stew, hot and warm and full of beans, and a rainbow salad which is bright in colour, and an orange fizzy drink. It's all delicious.

I eat so fast like I haven't eaten in days. Oh, I haven't.

It already feels more like Christmas here with a few decorations hanging on the stall fronts. But, disappointingly, there are still no stalls selling anything festive.

The streets of Seville are very busy. Restaurant tables line narrow pavements, almost sitting in the road, and it's difficult to get my suitcase around all the people. There's a buzz in the air; this is where I am going to spend Christmas, in Seville.

I find my hotel fairly easily. Hotel Abanico, on another narrow road in the old town. It's bland from the outside, and has a very colonial feel, yet it is beautifully decorated inside.

An open plan area is centred in the middle with tasteful seating scattered around which, I am assuming, was once an outdoor area where guests could look up to the sky. Arched windows stand high on the two floors above me too. It's stunning.

When I check in, the receptionist knows that I want a kettle. It's still in its box so he takes it out and hands it to me. I smile to myself in the lift on the way to my room.

There, I make a flask of tea with the kettle and eat my cake, but I am still excited to explore Seville, so I put the rest of the tea in my flask and go out. I don't want to waste a moment. Plus, it's only about an hour till my walking tour, where I am meeting the rest of the group at a location that made me want to come to Seville in the first place, Plaza de España.

When I get there, however, it's not quite how I pictured it, although nothing ever is. It's not as detailed as I thought it would be and yet, at the same time, it's even more impressive. The ceramic tiles are not so prominent, and I was so keen to see beautiful tiles. It's just careful photography which I will probably do as well. And there are lots and lots of tiles, it's just not as I expected it. But the whole Plaza de España is far bigger and much more inspiring. So, on the whole, I am really impressed. This place has a lovely atmosphere as well, with people milling about. Because it's spread out over such a large area, it doesn't feel crowded.

Even so, being here is a bit of a sensory overload, and it's difficult to process it all. Especially after all the images in my head already from Ronda and Setenil. I have gone from living a dull life, working and hibernating in my cold caravan, to whizzing around Andalucia. It's such a huge contrast.

I have not fallen in love with Seville instantly like I did in Ronda. It's actually a huge shock. This is a big city and Ronda was a small town, so they are going to be very different. So many big buildings, as you would expect, but the grandeur catches me out. Thousands of people scatter every street.

I find my walking group and sign in. There are ten of us and the guide is called Marina.

She starts by explaining the history of the building we're standing beside and I learn it was built much more recently than I thought, completed in 1928. Its long, magnificent outer walls fold around a semi-circle framing the area and four bridges cross a man-made river dotted with boats. The bit I was keen to see here are the 48 beautifully tiled benches, one for each province in Spain, all laid out alphabetically.

We continue our walk to the university building that used to be a tobacco factory. It has a huge deep moat, which is very unusual around a building. The moat was built because tobacco was extremely valuable, and there is also an underground passage for boats to come in safely from the river.

The tobacco was hand crushed to start with, then made

into cigarettes, and the men couldn't do this so they employed women with daintier fingers who only got 15 percent of the men's wages until they started striking. They then got better deals – working 13-hour days instead of 16. I would have walked past this building and not known any of that.

Hotel Alfonso XIII is our next stop, apparently the best hotel in Seville. All kinds of people stay here and it's certainly a stunning hotel.

You can get a cup of tea inside too, as they let riff raff in. Interestingly, it's owned by the council and they let it out for ten years at a time to a hotel chain. If you're successful in leasing it for ten years, you are not allowed to change its name and it must stay a hotel. I like this idea.

As we move on from the hotel, I try to talk to our tour guide about Christmas and the decorations here, explaining that I can't find any shops to buy a souvenir to take home.

She tells me that the emphasis in Spain is the Belén, which is the name for the Nativity scenes, and that sometimes she decorates her home and sometimes she doesn't.

It's a different attitude to England where some families put up their decorations on the 1st of December, inside and outside the house – complete with tree, hanging decorations, tinsel-covered staircases with it all wrapped around the bannisters, and boxes of Christmas decorations coming down from the loft scattered all over the house. English people can't wait to decorate. Here, they sometimes do and sometimes don't. I need to find out more.

In between points of interest, I try to chat to my fellow walkers who are a random bunch of people as always on a walking tour, asking them about their experience of Christmas in Spain as I am so keen to learn. I didn't think I would have to drag Christmas thoughts out of people. I thought it would all be here, to observe and witness, but I am having serious trouble finding out anything.

One lad is studying in Madrid, he doesn't know anything about Christmas here either, and he is from Canada which I don't know anything about but he doesn't offer anything.

It seems that no one knows or is even that interested about

Christmas in Spain. Two stories, however, come out of me begging everyone for information. One lady thinks there is a tradition to do with 12 grapes being eaten under the table; she can't remember much except she thinks it's for New Year.

Another lady talks about the Nativity scene, the Belén. She says that the Baby Jesus is missing until Christmas Day which I think is cute and proper if you are going to do this Nativity thing seriously.

It has made me wonder why, in England, it is all about the decorations and hardly about the Nativity. This so far seems the most startling difference. However, I don't think it's purely to do with religion. In my experience, everyone in England decorates their homes at this time of year, no matter if you are religious or not. It's not a choice where one excludes the other. Maybe if there is less going on at Christmas, like in Spain, then when you get to my age and it's changed, there is less to miss?

What I have struggled with is (what is quite comically called) 'empty nest syndrome' which sounds ridiculous and cute all at the same time. Like a little bird up in a tree when all the baby birds have flown away.

My nest full of chicks is not just empty, but it fell out of the tree. I don't live in the family home anymore, the nest. I don't have a house full of empty bedrooms, the family home is long gone. This is both a blessing and a sadness. A blessing because that sounds painful having a large house and empty bedrooms where your children used to be, and sad because all I ever wanted in life was a family home that my children could return to. However, my life didn't happen like that. I had to leave the family home and rent a house. So there isn't an empty nest but almost a yearning for one that my children could return to when they do come home.

This is complicated because, if I did still have the loving home, would I be even sadder in it without the children? My dream when I got married was to have a family home, a lovely husband, and a great marriage. Isn't that what everyone hopes for when they say 'I do'? That hasn't been the reality which also makes me sad, especially when my children come home and they don't have both parents living together. I feel for them as my dad left when I was 13, so I understand the pain. In an ideal world, I would still be married to their dad and it would be like the Waltons. But life isn't always like that.

I think maybe it's not Christmas that makes me exclusively sad, it's any time that my children come home to visit and that the 'nest' is now a caravan, which isn't how I pictured it.

Maybe I need to stop blaming Christmas for my empty nest issues. I still have lots to think through and plenty of time on this trip to work on it.

With the rest of the group, I keep going even though it's now dark. I have no idea where I am until Marina explains that the huge – and I mean huge – cathedral before us was once a mosque, now the biggest gothic cathedral in the world. I haven't decided yet if I want to go in.

There are so many orange trees along the streets and some have lights wrapped around them, twinkling through the leaves. I have only seen two proper Christmas trees so far, one in a shop in Ronda and the other in a hotel we just walked past. Marina says there is an orange wine that we should try which is made with these Seville oranges and it's very good.

We stop afterwards at the Giralda bell tower. Standing at 103 metres high, it started as a mosque, and now it isn't; a strong theme here. And, being a mosque, someone had to get to the top and shout for prayer five times a day, so apparently they installed 34 ramps for donkeys to transport people to the top.

The Giralda is stunning lit up against the black sky, its intricate details carved into the stone. It didn't have bells when it was a mosque but, later, 24 were added and it is now Christian.

Marina recommends that, if we have time on another day, we visit the Salvador church since we are now on our way to the Alcázar, and I am lucky enough to have a ticket for that tomorrow. We can't see anything at the Alcázar except a large Roman wall, apparently the beauty is inside. I am very excited to visit tomorrow.

The tour ends and I can see that none of us could have gone to any more locations. We are all worn out, this tour has taken nearly three hours. I am not sure it's been worth three hours of my life but it has given me a background to Seville, a bit of geography, and I learnt things that I would never have known otherwise which is why I love a good walking tour.

Despite the dark, the streets are very busy with hordes of people meandering slowly. It's like coming out of a train station, full of pushchairs, old people, families, couples. I never thought it would be this busy, not in the evenings in December. I can't move freely, instead I'm trapped behind people. Up ahead, I see some market stalls that look temporary. Maybe this is the Christmas market? If it is, then lovely, I can look for some decorations.

Eventually, I reach the stalls but … hmm.

I am so confused. There are two long rows of wooden stalls, about 20 of them, with glass fronts and openings to talk to the stall holders. As far as I can see though, the only things being sold are Nativity scenes. Above one is the word Belén. I look at each one, hoping for a Christmas stall that looks familiar. People are engaged looking at them, studying them, talking and discussing before they buy. Unfortunately, I don't get it.

I do get the idea of having one Nativity scene in your home, but surely once you have one you don't need another?

On closer inspection, and after a long walk up and down trying to work out what is happening, I think I do get it. Because this isn't the typical scene that I am familiar with; Mary, Joseph and a crib with a baby all in bright colours. In my experience, the Nativity scene is a token gesture that doesn't mean anything more than a fabric Father Christmas or a snowman hanging off a shelf.

These nativities look very real. The people look authentic, wearing the right clothes in the right colours, the donkeys look dirty, and other animals – the camels, sheep, and chickens – are surrounding the stable. There are carts for the donkeys to pull, kings, plants, trees, streams, workmen making things. Everything is in muted colours, making it so realistic. I can feel the straw and the atmosphere. I haven't seen anything like it before.

But I am disappointed there's no Christmas decorations, I just wanted a souvenir to take home. But I shouldn't be so discouraged, this is why I am travelling to find out what happens in other countries. This is a different culture, and maybe these Beléns make more sense than gold and green tinsel and tree decorations. I really don't know.

I turn a corner, meeting another row of stalls, and, yes, they have more Nativity scenes, all busy with people buying. It doesn't look like I am going to get any decorations.

Defeated, I enter my hotel into Google Maps and find my way home past the hordes of people, finally putting my bag in my room and heading down to the lounge area, the lovely open space in the middle.

I love this 18th century hotel. Spanish music plays as I sit on a beautiful teal settee and I can't take my eyes off all the décor, the little balconies on the floors above flowing with greenery, the arches on this level matching those on the first and second floor. I know now the arches are for the walkways to get to your room. A beautiful display of flowers sits on a table in front of me and my eyes can't keep from taking in all the details.

As I read the drinks menu, I think I might have a little treat and when I see they sell orange wine, well, I must try some. I ask the man at reception for some and he leads me through an arch to an absolutely stunning tiled room where he shows me all the complimentary drinks that I can help myself to all day for free. Tea, coffee, soup packets and orange wine, Vino Naraja. He shows me the bottle which he says is made exclusively for this hotel and pours me a tiny shot glassful to try. The plaque behind the wine bottle says 'the sweet wine is made with dehydrated skins from the famous bitter oranges of Seville'. He also offers me a biscuit wrapped in white paper that I have seen in all the shops and tells me proudly that it's made with pork, which sounds horrendous.

I take one anyway out of curiosity, politeness, and for research.

I do remember when booking this hotel that they did free coffees and teas but I thought it was just for the afternoons and that it might help me be sociable, that I could mingle with the other people staying here. But it looks like I am drinking alone.

However, it's lovely that I can drink free orange wine made from the oranges on the streets. I am just beginning to understand that you don't actually eat them, you make them into something else. I can't think of anything more significant to do in Seville right now than to drink orange wine from a famous Seville orange.

I sit on the gorgeous teal sofa next to the loveliest coffee table I have ever seen. It's like a big round bowl, a bit like the one I had soup in earlier, but a hundred times its size, with three chunky ornate legs and a glass top. I am not usually keen on glass topped tables but this one has an arrangement of lemons inside. They are nestled amongst greenery as if they were just taken off the tree. It's like something from a design magazine.

The wine is OK, it's more like sherry – sweet and thick – but nicer. Yes, I can drink this, although the biscuit is weird and I can't even finish it. The packaging is cute too. It was good to taste a traditional Seville Christmas biscuit. It's also good that I don't like it because they are free and, otherwise, I might be tempted to eat too many.

No one else is in here, so there's no socialising but I can enjoy my chill time and it feels like this is my home. I would love a house like this, it's so peaceful compared to the insanity out there in the centre of Seville.

After my first, I have a second shot glass of Seville orange wine which might be a mistake. I resist having a third, which I could easily do, it's very drinkable.

I have to remember that I haven't eaten anything since 3.00 pm.

Then I go up the gorgeous stairs to bed.

Sunday 24th December

It's Christmas Eve and I am very keen to go downstairs to see what the breakfast options are. My head knows that it had some alcohol last night, although it might be a touch of dehydration as well.

I walk across the beautiful landing from my room and look down at the area I was sitting in last night. On this level, there are full length doors that lead to nowhere unless you want to jump downstairs. To protect you from doing that, little iron railings are secured to stop you falling. I love the openness of these courtyards, the arches and the tiled floor.

Once at the bottom, off the small, tiled room that I was in yesterday where I got my orange wine from, I make my way to another room, decorated just as exquisitely. The breakfast is all laid out on the counter and it's a lovely selection, much better than I thought it would be, which is great as I am here for four nights.

I choose a big bowl of fruit and some bread with seeds and cheese, a boiled egg, tea, and juice, and afterwards feel happy and full. A few people are having breakfast in this room too, but all five of them are French. I was hoping to interact more with people today but it's not going to happen which is disappointing. I wanted to find out what people are doing for Christmas food tomorrow too, but I haven't had a conversation yet with anyone here. It is harder being solo when everyone else is in couples, it feels even more isolating when it's Christmas time. As if only saddos would travel on their own when it's obviously a family time and that must make me look even more dodgy. I came away to be open to any kind of Christmas Day, so if it's quiet, that's what it is.

I finish my food and get some green tea to take out to the little tables in the central area and write up my journal. I am purposely not rushing anywhere today as I want to enjoy this hotel and catch up with my Seville planning. I need to decide if I want to go to the cathedral and check that there are even any tickets available as it's Christmas tomorrow.

Today at one o'clock, I have a pre-booked ticket to visit the Alcázar which I am looking forward to. It's also called the Real Alcázar de Sevilla, or the Royal Alcázar of Seville.

I was worried about where to meet the guide for this as, yesterday, I saw very long queues and I don't want to be in the wrong place at the wrong time. But I have just received an email with instructions where to meet someone with a blue umbrella so that reassures me. I don't need to get there an hour early and fret.

I ask the man at reception about the rooftop bars here as that's something I want to do and I've already seen some recommendations in a book from my room, and on Facebook pages, but I want to see if the same name comes up. He points out a wooden mushroom attraction that I haven't seen yet. Look at me, I haven't been here 24 hours yet.

It's 11.00 am. now and as my tour is in two hours I am going to walk to the mushroom thing. I have chilled for quite a bit now. I try to use my map to find the way but get lost and have to turn Google Maps on. According to that, it should take eight minutes and now it's twelve, so I am going the wrong way.

I abandon it. I should have brought my sunglasses but didn't think to because it's December. As I keep exploring, I realise I am loving walking about up and down the lanes in the Jewish Quarter, and surprisingly, I am not completely lost. I have worked out where I am on the map by now. Some of these lanes are very narrow, reminding me of Venice a little. The first floors of the buildings along these streets have iron balconies, just wide enough to open the windows and not fall out. There isn't room in the lane for two balconies opposite each other, or they would be touching. Instead, in the tiny space, plants dangle down through the railings and make the street really attractive. There are many photo opportunities here.

Not long after this street, I arrive in a park where the sun is out and the sky is blue again. It feels like a spring day. There are Flamenco dancers here, and I am really happy. What more could I want on Christmas Eve in Seville?

This really is a treat. Lots of people are watching in front of a huge building, the wall painted orange making it a great backdrop. The first thing I notice is that the dancers are not dressed flamboyantly. The first wears a white blouse and a long black skirt, and the second wears a red dress but not the fluffy, layered, over-the-top dress that comes to mind when I think of Flamenco dancing.

They stand on a board tapping their feet with great passion to the sound of a man playing the guitar. They dance like their life depends on it, throwing absolutely everything they have into the performance, their arms so descriptive, expressive, and energetic, their faces full of the words they aren't saying. And, all the while, supported by a guitarist and a man who claps enthusiastically, occasionally singing.

Standing in the sunshine watching this outdoor performance is mesmerising and the whole experience of being here in Seville, watching them, gives me goosebumps.

I tear myself away after dropping some coins in their hat.

Following my little detour, I find where I need to be and, by now, really need a wee. Urgently now, so I walk into a friendly looking tapas bar and confidently go up to the bar. I spot the loo and head straight for it, then come out again and look at the tapas – if I have to buy something, I will, as I do have 20 minutes to spare, but the staff don't even look at me so I leave.

Now, I am sitting in the Plaza del Triunfo in the sunshine. I spot the blue umbrella I've been told to look out for and show them my ticket, then get given a radio to hang round my neck.

But, oh no, the tour guide explains to our group that, as the Alcázar is a royal residence, security needs to see ID, a passport or driving licence. My passport is at the hotel.

Drat.

Thankfully, she says a photo will do. I remember going through my photos, deleting old ones before I came away, and saw a photo of my passport and nearly deleted it but didn't. I thought it would be a good idea to keep in case I do lose it and still have the details.

I frantically search through the photos on my phone and find it. Thank goodness.

We go through security, relieved they're happy with my photo, and have our bags scanned like we are an airport. I admit, I'm a little impatient. This is eating into our time and the ticket was expensive.

Once we're ready, the tour guide starts by telling us that this palace was built to show off. As well as a palace, there are extensive gardens, and gardens need water and water is valuable – the idea being that if you have extensive gardens it shows you are wealthy. She shows us an old aqueduct that used to bring the water into the garden in the 11th century. By the 13th century, the Muslims were out and Christians were in. She seems quite flippant about this but maybe she has accepted this history. For me, having very little knowledge of it, these power struggles sound awful.

We learn that the palace has had a mish-mash of different owners from different cultures over the last thousand years. Each different historical period added a different style, so there are Gothic, Renaissance, Baroque, Islamic and Christian influences. I can't wait to go in.

Before us, three main palaces would've led off from the courtyard we are standing in, but there was a serious earthquake once and so one was ruined.

Our guide tells us that one palace was made by the same person who built the Alhambra in Granada as a gift to his friend, and that he was the first Christian to see the Alhambra and cried with joy.

We step inside and I am blown away.

The room we are standing in is called Sala de la Justicia and my description is not going to do it any justice, so perhaps google it. The room is square and the walls are filled with intricate details, it's difficult to tear your eyes away. It is so detailed that it reminds me of fine lace, but it's plaster, decorated with the tiniest raised patterns and lots of arches.

I let my eyes adjust and take in the wooden ceiling, the rich dark wood such a contrast to the pale plasterwork, stunning in its own right. The domed roof boasts geometric patterns, giving the whole room a more theatrical feel.

We move through the palace to another area, they all flow easily from one to the other. In a centred patio area, the tour guide points out the tiling, where a woman is holding a bunch of flowers, the symbol of a woman being at her best, blooming and at her most fertile, which is why brides hold flowers. I never knew that. Isn't life strange? What would modern women who choose not to have children feel about holding flowers implying they are at their peak and ready to reproduce?

We go into King Pedro's windowless bedroom, decorated in lots of blue and green showing his wealth. I do wonder, though, that if anyone got as far as the king's bedroom would they really care about the colours?

Next, we find ourselves in the outdoor patio that you see in a lot of photos of the Alcázar of Seville, the Patio de las Doncellas, so it feels a bit familiar as I was expecting to see this bit. The oblong patio has a water feature running down the centre and arches stand proudly all the way round. These arches carry on with this detailed plaster work which you can't help photographing.

I think I must be almost done with so much sensory overload in this place until I see some absolutely stunning arches with hints of blue and decide that, so far, these are my favourite. The blue emphasises the details on the plaster, making it even more spectacular. The ceiling is again wooden and a thing of beauty all on its own with its deep, rich colour, the symmetrical patterns, and so much attention to detail. The ceilings in my opinion are as beautiful and magnificently crafted as the arches and the intricate plaster work.

Every room has a different ceiling and you would be hard pressed to pick a favourite. It's mind blowing. I take a lot of photos and really hope they capture the beauty of it. As we keep going, there are more rooms and more photos and more wows but all I can say is go and book a plane ticket to go and see it all for yourself.

The last room is the Salón de Los Embajadores, the Ambassadors' Hall. I can't say it's the best room, I don't think you can pick just one room as I have loved details from all of them, but this has to be up there as one of the most impressive. It has a stunning, very high gold ceiling and the four walls creating its square design are covered across every single inch with intricate plaster work. It's ornate, spectacular, over the top, intricate, skilful, elaborate and just, wow.

The guide explains some of the history behind the shapes and the symbols but I don't really care. I am just enjoying being here and I can't take in any more facts.

There's a quietness to this room as everyone is trying to process what they are seeing and my neck hurts from looking up.

It's all very overwhelming.

The décor changes now as we enter the Capilla del Palacio Gótico, the Chapel of the Gothic Palace. We're told the yellow tiles come from Portugal and that this building is made of stone and not tiny bricks, so it is more substantial.

This, we're also told, was a wedding room and the tiles show the bride and groom. The bride has a really big forehead – I am not being rude, apparently it was fashionable. A big forehead meant that you had a big brain and were intelligent and intelligence was sexy. So, on her wedding day, she actually shaved some of her hair to make her forehead look even bigger so that she looked even more attractive. So unusual to remember that fashions have been with us for a very long time. I hope this one doesn't come full circle, I don't think I would want to take part.

The tiled floor has dance steps in the pattern, for those who had too much to drink and didn't know where to put their feet.

And that's the end of the tour. It's good to get out into the sunshine and the gardens – that was a lot to take in and it's going to stay with me for a long time. A wander round the garden will let my brain relax.

I consider getting a drink and a snack until I see the prices, so keep walking.

The gardens are stunning, especially when it's as warm as a spring day, and I see as much as I can before sitting down to relax for a bit.

After a little while, I notice two Germans who were on the same tour as me with vegan badges pinned to their bags, so I chat with them to get some good food recommendations. It's time to leave, I have been here for hours.

I decide to go to the restaurant Naturalmente, which they recommended to me. The food is delicious but expensive and not very filling. The two Germans must have had more money than me and ordered more food than I did. I thought one meal would fill me up, but it hasn't.

Now it's time to visit the mushroom structure. They have a few names for it here; Metropol Parasol Seville or Las Setas de Sevilla.

When I arrive at the mushroom attractions, I immediately think they are weird. I was looking forward to seeing this but, to be honest, I find them quite offensive. I am sure they have divided opinions in Seville.

Whether this is because I am now at the complete other end of the scale when it comes to things to do in Seville, or whether my reaction would have been the same if I had visited these first, I will never know. But they couldn't be more different. You can't compare something that was built in the 11th century, that has evolved over different cultures, to a huge wooden thing that was built in 2011. I simply can't understand why it was ever made.

Firstly, these structures don't in my opinion look anything like mushrooms, not that they were supposed to, I don't think, it's just a nickname. The huge spiralling wooden structure looks fluid and has been built in what must have once been a lovely historic square. I am going to google what it looked like before this happened and I bet that it looked better. I understand cities need to move forward with ideas and find new ways to impress the tourists, but this tourist is not impressed.

Apparently, it costs €15 to walk across the top. I would actually like to see the views from the top but, if I pay to do that, I have said that I agree with it and I don't.

Instead, I start to walk back to the hotel, popping into a bakery on the way where a man in front of me accidentally spills his coffee all over the floor. While mopping up is under way, I must speak Spanish as I can't go to the cabinet and point at what I want. Amazingly, I come out with the right cake.

When I get back to the hotel, I enjoy an hour's rest with a big flask of tea and cake, trying to work out what else I want to do in Seville.

A rooftop bar, I think, is what I will do next.

I walk to the cathedral and look out for a bar called Em. As soon as I find it, there's a security guard at the bottom. I ask him if I can go up, and he asks if I am one person. I say yes, does he think I am with the invisible man? Obviously, I am on my own.

I reach the fourth floor by a lift and find this is a modern, trendy bar full of couples a whole lot younger than me. I scan the QR code as I can at least do that, I am not that old.

And I nearly fall over at the price. I was going to have a mocktail, but not at €13, and it's €16 for something yummy with alcohol. I almost go back down, then see wine for €7 which is expensive for Spain but not horrific for a rooftop bar looking at the cathedral.

I do have to admit, however, it's a great spot. I am directly opposite the cathedral and the Giralda tower lights up slowly as the sun goes down. This is such a simple thing to do but very enjoyable as I watch the sun setting over Seville. The wine is delicious and I even get a little bowl of nibbles.

It's a lovely experience. Sometimes I think I try to cram too much in when I travel but I enjoy the variety. I have had so many different experiences today and this is the perfect end to

Christmas Eve in Seville.

I decide that before I go back to the hotel, I want to go to Plaza de España before it gets too late so I can see it in the dark. It's quite a long walk but worth it to see it lit up. The ceramic tiles look really pretty, shining in the night lights, the water so still and reflective. The bridges are stunning; I take some lovely photos.

It's a long walk back and I am tired now. I still don't really like being out at night so I stomp home fast across the centre of Seville.

On my return, I drop my things off at my room and go down to the lovely chair. It feels like my chair as I haven't seen anyone else in this area yet, then settle down with a shot glass of orange wine and a mint tea. I don't want a headache and this is a good combination.

I scroll through the photos I've taken today, uploading some to Facebook, and chat to the receptionist about Christmas. I really want to learn some more but it's like pulling teeth trying to get any information.

I ask him why there aren't any signs of Christmas in the hotel as there isn't a tree or any decorations. He says the owners don't think the room needs Christmas decorations as it's already lovely. I quite agree that it's lovely, that is a fact, but it does show you that Christmas decorations are just not a priority here. I also think that the floral display is almost as big as a small tree so one could have gone right there on the table, but it's not my hotel.

I ask him what Spanish people do in their homes. He explains about the Belén. Some houses have big Nativity scenes and no decorations, some no Nativity and lots of decorations. Some both, depending on the individual's faith.

He keeps asking me if I want to go and eat Japanese food, as it's open, and I realise he must know the owners.

While I sit on my sofa, I hear him checking more people in, telling everyone about the Japanese place. He says only Arabic, Buddhist and Japanese places will be open for food tomorrow, so my Christmas dinner should be interesting.

In the meantime, I decide to book a ticket for the cathedral to visit on Boxing Day. It's €16 which is too much, but I have been to the Sagrada Família in Barcelona, Burgos Cathedral, and Leon Cathedral, so I might as well go here too. And it lets me into the Salvador church which I think is baroque.

So, at almost 24,000 steps today, it's time for bed. I shower and wash my clothes Camino style.

Monday 25th December

It's Christmas Day and I am not sure how I am supposed to be feeling, having never run away to Spain before. I open my tall wooden shutters and hang out my wet clothes on the railings because they haven't even started to dry yet. It's an unusual way to start Christmas.

I walk down the stairs to the gorgeous, tiled breakfast room for a Spanish hotel Christmas breakfast. This feels very strange, like I have stepped out of life and re-created a parallel universe. It feels much stranger than I thought it would, avoiding Christmas in England.

Four French people are here for breakfast too. I am about to say, 'Feliz Navidad,' when one of the ladies say, 'Bonjour,' before they all get up and leave, and it's just me.

Oh well, Happy Christmas to me.

I picked this hotel because it looked social but you can't obviously know how social the guests will be, or their nationality. Perhaps I should have gone to a hostel for Christmas instead of an expensive hotel. But that might have been awful as hostels are very unpredictable. I might have been in a noisy dorm with messy twenty-somethings, who drank a lot. But at least someone would have said, 'Happy Christmas,' and it would have been social even if I didn't like it.

This is a very strange situation I have found myself in. Not found myself in, I created this situation, and I am not quite sure if it was the right one.

The TV hanging on the wall is talking about energy prices which isn't really adding to the Christmas vibes. In fact, there is absolutely nothing Christmassy about today so far, not one piece of Christmas decoration anywhere in the hotel, and no people to talk to. Breakfast is the same as yesterday and probably the same as tomorrow. I haven't got any cards or gifts, or given any.

This is about as un-Christmassy as you can possibly get.

But I am OK with that, I think. It's just unusual.

On the TV, one man is being interviewed, sitting in the sunshine with a shirt on, saying that it's too cold at home and he can't afford to heat it. This makes me laugh, not for the man who thinks he is cold but because the Spanish don't know how lucky they are. He should try living in Cornwall in the winter, and trying to heat a home, then he will know what cold is.

Through the doorway, a new couple comes into the dining room. The man is Scottish, so speaks English, though the woman doesn't say anything. We chit chat a little but not much. I think people are wary of single people here. I try not to be offended.

I am quite used to re-creating Christmas, as it hasn't always been celebrated the traditional way in my life with my children. Since 2020 when me, Aidan and Jamie handed back the keys to our rented house, we celebrate Christmas as a family in November or December, depending on if my sister is over from America and Liam and Ciara get back to Cornwall if they are not in France or Germany. I pay for an Air BnB and we all meet there, some of us staying the night, and we exchange gifts. As I can't cook a traditional roast since it's never my kitchen and I don't have all my kitchen things, we order Chinese food instead to be delivered to the house.

The advantage of doing it this way is that now the children, who are not children anymore, can do their own thing on Christmas Day. It takes away any complicated loyalties that they might have. They can spend Christmas with their other halves, or even their other halves' families, and not feel bad that they haven't seen me because we have already celebrated.

It does work, and we enjoy it, but it's all over too quickly once we pack our bags and leave the Air BnB. I am happy that we have found a way of doing Christmas even if it's not ideal, but I would like it to be longer.

So today, although it's Christmas Day, and I am not at home, it's not as if I have abandoned my children. I haven't left them to it and run away, there was nothing to run away from because I was never going to see them today. I was never going to have all my children around a big table and cook a huge roast dinner.

That hurts on many levels but it's also very normal. A lot of families disperse once their children become adults. I need to adjust to it, embrace the freedom, which I am doing physically, I just need my emotions to catch up.

We also used to move Christmas Day when the children were small. My mum organised the Salvation Army Christmas dinner because she worked in the kitchen of a day centre. It was held at her workplace on Christmas Day, so we just moved our celebrations to Boxing Day and did everything as you would, only the date on the camcorder showed the wrong date.

Life changes, children grow up and get on with their own lives just as they should, but it doesn't mean that I don't miss those times when they were small.

In fact, I wonder if that's it, that Christmas without my children isn't Christmas anymore and it never will be. They are never going to be aged seven, nine and ten again, and I have to accept that. I almost need to grieve that, because it feels like a loss, something that happened and it's over. I still have my children and I am grateful they have grown into amazing adults but it can't ever be as it was. It's gone and I must replace it with something else. Maybe once I have figured that out, I will feel at peace with Christmas.

If there were grandchildren, it would have made the transition easier, but there isn't. That would have filled this void, this emptiness. I have had conversations with my children explaining that they must never feel obligated to give me grandchildren. Times have changed so much – when I grew up, I just knew I wanted to have a family, it wasn't even something I consciously thought about. I didn't ever ask myself if it was what I wanted because I knew that it was. But the children these days are different. They are questioning parenthood and whether it's something that they want to do.

I have also admitted to them that if I had stopped and weighed up all the pluses and minuses of having children, I might not have had any. My children are OK with me saying that. With parenthood comes a constant worry for your children, and a fear of them getting hurt or distressed, which I sometimes find overwhelming.

I have tried to explain what it's like having children to people who haven't yet. In my opinion, you feel the highs and lows of your children's lives far more intensely than you do your own. If they are struggling or in pain, you feel even worse than they do. If they hurt, you hurt even more. When they have their hearts broken in relationships, then you hurt too. If they hurt physically, you want to take that pain away from them.

On the other hand, if they are happy, you are happy too. Your children are precious. You have given birth to them, sacrificed parts of yourself, given up years of your life for their existence. So, if they do well in a swimming competition, draw an amazing picture, or dance on a stage then you feel so happy that your heart could melt with joy.

So if you want to make your life far more emotional with huge highs and lows, have children. When you have children, they open doors into areas that you might not have gone to. Different work choices and different places to live which enrich your own life.

If I hadn't had children, I wouldn't have stayed in a bad marriage. Although I absolutely don't want my children to feel any responsibility for that. I would have far more money, because children are expensive, and I didn't have a career. I would have travelled more, I would have been a brilliant aunt to my nieces.

But, would I have been content? I don't know because I never lived that life. All I do know is that, despite the restrictions, fear and selflessness, it has also brought me such a lot of joy. Joy that you can't quantify, or put into words.

So, maybe Christmas is just the 25th of December and that's what I need to accept. It's just a day.

After breakfast, I go out for a stroll. This is the first Christmas Day in my life where I can do exactly what I want to do. I don't have much planned, I am just going to see what happens.

The streets near the hotel are empty. It's frosty again and the church bells are ringing. I haven't beaten the crowds to Plaza de España but I suppose 10.00 am. is not that early and it's actually nice to see so many people.

The sun is shining at one end of the plaza and so everyone is getting in each other's way, trying to take that perfect photo at the sunny end. It's a lot of fun, everyone is enjoying themselves. After taking loads of photos, I wander about, happy with a full belly and no agenda.

The sound of music starts up and dancing appears under one of the arches of the huge curved building before me, revealing a male Flamenco dancer. I haven't seen a male Flamenco dancer before and I wasn't expecting to see one today, so this is a nice treat. Already, he has pulled in quite a crowd and he is very good, just as passionate as the female dancers in the park. He knows the camera is on him, enjoying the attention, and a singer accompanies him. I can't understand a word but enjoy the whole performance.

Eventually, I tear myself away.

I decide I am going to see if I can get into the five-star Hotel Alfonso XIII for a drink as Marina suggested. I walk in, delighted to see a beautiful Christmas tree, a wonderful sight on Christmas Day, and only the third one I have seen in Spain. The staff let me in and I speak in Spanish, even though the receptionist says hello in English. I have to be confident and keep practising.

In the centre of the hotel is a beautiful outdoor courtyard with a water fountain. This might be where they put the riff raff. The seating is spaced out and very comfortable, full of iron chairs with cushions and glass-topped tables. The entire courtyard is square-shaped with arches all the way round, showing off lots of detail, and the building is similar in style to the Alcázar with its arches and tall ceilings, a stunning balcony area located on the first floor. The stone and sand colours are gorgeous as well, with touches of blue and the black iron miniature balconies. A small orange tree stands in each corner.

I order a green tea with no idea how much it will cost but I don't care. It is what it is. I am experiencing five-star luxury and I am going to enjoy it.

I open up Facebook on my phone while I wait for my tea. It is so full of Christmas, it feels like I am watching it from another planet. Phil is busy cooking a full roast, and still opening presents. Our lives are very different today and that's good. This is what I wanted.

I can't say that I am not enjoying myself here in Spain. I am enjoying all the new sights, the experiences, and the weather but I am definitely going to miss a roast dinner, one of my favourite meals. I am missing the English traditions, the things that make this day what it is. A tree, heavily decorated with mementos from all our many Christmases. a big roast that you start cooking in the morning that takes all day; gifts, chocolates, and that lazy feeling of just indulging the whole day through.

But I am in Spain in a five-star hotel, and life is OK.

I still don't know what I am paying for this tea, but it's divine which makes me happy. Delicious, top-quality loose leaf green tea in the cutest teapot, and another pork biscuit with Phil's name on it because I am not eating it.

I chill, breathe out, and enjoy this. What a unique way to spend Christmas morning, chilling in an open-air courtyard in a very tasteful five-star hotel with the best cup of green tea I've had out in years. I have discovered from travelling that we make decisions and can end up in such wildly different places, often good, sometimes not. But occasionally you strike gold and everything is a delight.

Life is full of choices and gambles. You have to be brave, listen to advice, act on it, and be prepared to get turned away. I might not have gotten inside this hotel, but I did. If I hadn't gone on the walking tour I wouldn't have thought to come in.

I could have just walked past the hotel, thinking that I wasn't good enough. We are all good enough and deserve nice treats.

I wanted this Christmas to be different to break the sadness from missing my children. I wanted to avoid Christmas and yet, I am looking for it everywhere.

All my children have messaged me, except Ciara who I

know was up late last night in a different time zone in Ecuador, and so has my mum and Phil.

Everyone is fine.

My mum is probably not fine, but I have to live with that. She is home alone and I know that I shouldn't have left my 82 year-old mum on her own, obviously. But she could have gone to friends; she just prefers to be at home. My mum had three children. My sister lives in America and never sees our mum on Christmas Day since her children have grown up. She used to come over when they were small, but they are adults now living their own lives. My brother died in 2020 so he's not here for Christmas either.

Does that mean I should have filled the gap to be with her? Is it my responsibility?

Perhaps it is. But I think my mum understands why I am here, or at least knows this is what I want to do, which is similar. My mum probably misses our Christmases when the children were small as much as I do, but what can I do about it? I need to do my own thing but that guilt of being selfish creeps in all the time. If I was needed at home though, I would jump on the next flight.

I say, 'Feliz Navidad,' to the waiter, again feeling that need to talk about Christmas, to validate it, to try and feel it. He smiles so politely that I wonder if maybe it's not normal to say, 'Happy Christmas,' to people you don't know. There are so many cultures here and some of them don't celebrate today, so it's possibly not what I should have done.

People I met at the Alicante bench back in the Plaza de España spoke about Benidorm and I wished them a Happy Christmas, but they were British so that's OK.

The bill for my drink comes out after a little while in a pink padded folder. As casually as I can, I open it, trying to work out in advance what would be horrendous but it's €6.00. That's OK. It was a perfect cup of quality tea and well worth that. I keep the sugar sachet as it has the hotel on it. I even keep the receipt.

Why? To show off that I have been here or to save as a souvenir of a genuinely lovely pit stop. I don't know.

Sometimes I don't understand, I just do things.

Isn't money strange? Here, it apparently costs anything from €300 off-season to €3,000 a night to stay in this hotel. I can't imagine having that kind of money. And if I did, would I ever spend even €300 on a room for one night, never mind €3,000?

And why should money buy you better things? Is this better than my hotel? I don't think it is. I have gone to the top end of my budget for a special hotel for Christmas and I am happy with my choice.

On my trip to Ronda, I thought about the natural beauty of the place and I did spot a very well-dressed couple, you can just tell sometimes. Seeing them, I did wonder if they were having a better experience than me, or was it exactly the same? The beauty of the landscape was free for everyone to enjoy.

I suppose this hotel is a world that only money lets you into unless you sneak in for a cuppa. I am curious as to what I would have gotten for a €3,000 per night price tag? I would be surprised if my entire trip costs as much as that.

The toilets, however, aren't great. I walk back down the front steps of the hotel and out into Seville, dodging the trams. I would like to go on one but don't know how to buy a ticket or where I would go.

Wandering around shops feels very strange on a day like today. I have to stop thinking this is Christmas, because it's not. It's only the 25th of December in Seville. But as the shops are open, I might as well still look for a gift with Feliz Navidad on, although I know I will fail.

I walk across the bridge to the busy Triano district, full of people sitting outdoors at cafés eating and drinking. Not a lot of roasts being cooked here. When I think that probably 90 percent of the UK households are cooking a full Christmas dinner right now, surrounded by piles of wrapping paper, stuffed full of Quality Street, it seems funny that, here, everyone is just doing what they do every day.

Up ahead, I see a huge red church with people going in, so I follow.

But, oh dear, there's Mass going on and I've just

unknowingly gate crashed it. I quickly sit down, listening to the man in a white robe who looks tiny against the huge backdrop of the gold altar. It's a spacious church, the white painted walls and ceiling showing off the gold décor, and the congregation all start singing. It's very nice, even though I can't understand any of it.

The man at the altar then speaks passionately and I do make out some of the words as he gets his wine and rice paper circles out.

People drop to their knees to pray, luckily not everyone so I don't join in, but I am always ready to drop to my knees in a Catholic church – although I didn't know what faith this was when I walked in.

A lady comes round for the donations and I throw some coins in, since I am one of them at the moment, before we come to the bit where you shake your neighbour's hand. Luckily I know about this part as well and smile at everyone around me. They are too far away to actually shake hands, smiling will have to do. It's all quite bizarre.

When the man in the white robe turns his back to the congregation, I run out of the door onto the noisy street again, glad to have escaped yet still glad, in a way, that I did attend something religious on Christmas Day. A first for me.

I continue walking but nothing sparks my interests. A lot of shops are shut so I turn around and head home. I am very tired by now, it's been quite a morning.

Back at the hotel, I put my phone on charge and indulge in a cup of tea and the two cakes I took from breakfast. I ring my mum to wish her a Happy Christmas. She has been to Salvation Army service this morning, so she has seen people and she is now cooking herself a roast dinner.

Satisfied, I go down for another cuppa but again it's very quiet, so quiet that it feels like I am the only one staying here. No one is about down here but nice music is filtering through.

I research what to do when I leave Seville. I have two spare days with nothing planned before I get to Córdoba and look into the options, considering possibly Écija or Carmona.

Browsing Booking.com, I see there's nothing in Écija , so

search Carmona and find there's a nuns' convent which sounds like bliss after noisy, bustling Seville, costing €70 for two nights. I book it, knowing I will sort a bus out this evening.

It won't take long to get there, I think it said it's only 30 kilometres away, so what should I do with the rest of Christmas Day? It's only 4.00 pm.

I message Phil, he is still cooking his turkey with all the trimmings for his girls and his dad.

I would pay good money for a roast dinner right now. Something warm and comforting with some vegetables.

At 4.30 pm., I go off to explore more of the Jewish Quarter, full of tiny narrow streets that cars are trying to drive down, scratching their tyres on the kerbs when they don't quite fit. It's wonderful wandering with no agenda and no time limits.

Eventually, after another stern talk with myself, I decide that as it's Christmas I deserve a Christmas dinner – Spanish style – so head towards the cathedral. The restaurants are all open just like yesterday, busy with people sitting on tables at the front of restaurants. The man on reception was telling fibs. I walk up and down, looking at people's plates and the menus and, after having done a huge survey, sit down at a table with a good view of the bars and part of the cathedral. I've had my eyes on spinach and chickpea tapas and this menu has it.

I have the strangest dinner ever, let alone the fact I'm eating it on Christmas Day – a thick spinach and chickpea tapas in a bowl with a tiny cracker, gazpacho, and a glass of sangria. With a bread roll, it's delicious. To my left are English speaking people from California and, to their left, a family from London, chatting away.

I try to join in but, even amidst their busy chatter, I feel part of the group even if I wasn't.

All in all, it's been a successful Christmas dinner.

I have felt very chilled today, which doesn't happen usually on Christmas Day. They have, over the years, been incredibly stressful. Cooking a huge dinner for 11 sometimes, as well as breakfast, and opening gifts. Today I haven't cooked a thing.

It's half past six now, maybe it's time to go back.

In the lounge area back at the hotel, I sit in my usual spot with a mint tea and an orange wine. There's no one about again. I ring Phil, he tells me he had a lovely traditional Christmas.

Here, I am no nearer to finding out what Christmas in Spain is all about. I don't seem to have had Christmas at all.

And yet, I don't feel upset. I was preparing myself for some emotions today, but there weren't any. It's been four years now since my last Christmas Day with my children and mum so I am adjusting, it's a process.

I haven't had that Christmas feeling today. That feeling you can't identify but everyone talks about. It usually happens to me when I make mince pies. I think this is because I only ever make mince pies at Christmas when the decorations are up. My mum used to make them when I was a child, so the memory goes back to my childhood. They smell like Christmas when they are cooking and taste amazing. Far better than shop-bought ones. What I do love is that most Christmases my children ask me for the recipe again as they are making them which warms my heart. Taking the simple traditions forward into the next generation.

I tend to randomly miss my children, it doesn't happen on any particular days. Sometimes it just catches me out and it feels like my heart has been crushed, but that hasn't happened today.

It's quite freeing, not celebrating Christmas, and I should embrace that. I am free from society telling me what to do.

I can round my children up at any time of the year to be together, eat, play games, talk. Isn't that what life is about? I will do more of that. Next year, I will get them all together as often as I can.

This has been good for me going away, everything seems a little clearer now.

Tuesday 26th December

I had a broken night's sleep because the bin men were outside at 1.00 am. Surprising for Boxing Day.

All night, lots of people walked around chatting loudly and the roads outside are so narrow and windy, the buildings so tall, that the noises of vehicles driving past echoed. The wooden shutters at my window didn't really help at all.

Even so, I enjoy my third breakfast here and, afterwards, retreat to my room for a cup of tea as they only have tiny cups down there.

Today, I am struggling to get motivated. I look tired in the bathroom mirror. Shattered really, but that's not surprising. Málaga feels like a month ago.

I chill in my room, making sure to enjoy my cup of tea and spend some time practising speaking Spanish on my Duolingo app. I think it's getting a little easier being immersed in the sounds all around me. I got the gist of the news on the TV this morning reading the subtitles in Spanish, nowhere near even half of it but at least it's making a little more sense as time goes by.

Having already booked my ticket on Christmas Eve, I am going to visit the cathedral today, then the church and possibly a shopping centre if I can find it. I asked the man at reception where I can buy Christmas decorations and he gives me instructions, which is exciting.

I soon find the shop that he recommended and it's not a five-storey shopping centre but a big department store which is a shame. I wanted individual shops, some variety, and I don't see any decorations in the big store, so I leave.

Outside, there's a huge police presence in the street, with two policemen on horses, a large police van and another row of five policemen. One is holding a large gun poised, ready to go. They all look alert and serious and yet the people shopping don't look at all worried.

I don't like it here, I just wanted a decoration with Feliz

Navidad on it. How hard can that be?

I go down the pretty street with lovely looking Christmas lights even though they are not lit yet.

There are so many shops here, selling shoes, clothes, underwear, bags, and – ahh, books – all amid thousands of people.

Although it's pretty, I need to get out of this busy street of people carrying brown bags with shop logos on before I combust. I feel tired and irritable today; I am not giving Seville any more of my money.

Eventually, I arrive at an artisan market in a plaza with about 50 stalls. But no Feliz Navidad, just jewellery, scarves, jewellery, jewellery, more jewellery, and bags.

I should come back next Christmas with a stall. The English would buy a Feliz Navidad gift. The last stall is a proper artisan one, with handmade wooden carvings featuring tiny, gorgeous little buildings made from twigs and branches. Absolutely stunning but, at €120 each, I don't think so. I follow my paper map until I arrive at El Salvador Church and get in with my pre-paid ticket and, oh my. Peace at last, away from all that material goods on those shopping streets. I sit on a bench facing the altar and breathe out.

It's beautiful, big and spacious, with a gold and baroque style painting on the ceiling. I love it.

I don't know why churches make me feel peaceful, I can actually feel the tension leave my body, it's very physical. I am not religious so it's nothing to do with faith, but there is always an energy in a church. This one feels important and it's definitely recharging me.

I think it's the passion, the details, the art, vision, the stonemasons, and all that individual skill. People made this with their skills and vision, not with machinery or computers, and a long time ago in a world that I can't picture.

It's a privilege to sit down and enjoy it. There's an energy off the people in here as well, everyone is whispering out of respect, no one is talking at normal level.

The more I look around, the more I see, it's stunning. I get up and walk all the way around the church. The Nativity scene is beautiful, seeming so real, especially as the models are almost life sized. It's quite something. The carvings on the pillars are so detailed, the two sides facing the altar painted, while the other two are left as stone. I like both.

I relax, just sitting there, for an hour before heading back into the hustle and bustle, now much calmer.

I do feel that this Christmas in Spain has been about the Nativity. It's important here in the heart of Seville, far more important than Christmas decorations.

Outside in the streets again, I notice there's a huge queue for something, maybe a sale, so walk alongside it, surprised to find the line of people is about a quarter of a mile long. I reach the front where there's security on the door. I can just see inside, and I think it's another Nativity scene. I bet it must be good if the queue is this long, but I don't know if you need a ticket or how long it all takes and I have to get to the cathedral.

It's not a long walk back to get there. Inside the doors, a man hands me a radio guide, not saying anything, and I have no idea what to do. When I ask, he says, 'Tower first,' with no enthusiasm at all.

I follow the many people already here and walk up 34 ramps to the top. As we walk on the right, more people come down on the left. It's crowded and claustrophobic. The ramps are great though, better than steps, and I think about the donkeys who used to walk up here each day.

We keep climbing, meeting some congestion at the top as you would expect.

Gosh, this is awful, a big bottleneck of people all wanting to see the view. There are three areas to view from each side, with one under construction, and you have to walk up a few steps to look out. But, first, you have to wait your turn in the vague queuing system.

I get to look out of three sides, but can barely see a thing through the wire. I have had enough, and make my way back down.

It's a shame because, every time I see a photo of the Giralda, I will only think of 34 ramps going round and round now, full of tourists. I would prefer not to have done this. It feels like a real money spinner. There's no customer service at all, no information on my radio guide, and I have no idea what to do next.

Back near the bottom, I wander around the cathedral which is huge with its massive pillars, from floor to enormous ceiling. I have no idea which way to go and I can't see many numbers to put into my radio guide and, when I do, it's so dull and boring I don't want to listen.

The main gold altar is impressive but it's behind a steel gate and you have to look through the bars. I am disappointed as I love a cathedral. But I am not loving this one. I think I prefer the outside of it to the inside

After an hour, and that includes my walk to the top, I leave, unable to bear it anymore. I might be tired, but it's so emotionless in there, and as cold as the stone within it. There's no atmosphere at all, except apathy.

I need a cup of tea, so I go back to the hotel. It's 3.00 pm. now and I probably won't go out again. I have done everything that I wanted to do in Seville and more. I have enjoyed it but I do struggle with big cities; they wear me out much more than towns.

I chill in my room for a couple of hours, eat guacamole, hummus and crisps, and some chocolate from home that Aidan and his fiancée, Thea, bought me for our Christmas in November. Then I go down to my blue settee and get a mint tea. Checking my steps, I see that I have walked 72,000 steps in Seville. That's crazy.

Ciara messages me and shows me how to use Google Maps offline. I had no idea you could do this, so will try that out, and screenshot the nuns' convent for tomorrow anyway in case the offline maps don't work.

While I have free time, I also book a flight home. I really want to fly into Newquay in Cornwall as it will save me hours of travel time, so I book a flight for the 14th of January, almost three weeks away. How exciting, I have many more days to see new things.

It will be sad leaving this hotel with its beautiful décor and my blue settee. It's just a shame it wasn't more social here but that's OK. Maybe I would have been frustrated with too many people sharing this lovely space with me or sitting on my settee.

I chat to a man from Gibraltar for a few minutes, who I said hello to at breakfast this morning, then go upstairs to my room, have a shower and read my Kindle.

The youngsters next door must be watching a film and one has the most awful squealy laugh. It's nice that they are enjoying themselves but it's a very noisy laugh, and such a long film, that it starts to bother me.

It's only 10.15 pm. but the high-pitched laughter is piercing through me and I get up to go to the loo. They are even louder from here so they must be on the other side of this wall.

Before I think it through, I bang on the wall three times and they stop laughing. Suddenly, it's very quiet. I can imagine their faces on the other side and they do stay quiet for a while but then it starts again. The street below is very noisy too, cars going by, people shouting out in the tiny street, so I just have to put up with it.

I am tired and fall asleep.

Wednesday 27th December

I have my last breakfast by 7.45 am. and walk over to the bus station where a breakdown pick-up truck is towing a car. The pick-up truck itself is tiny, just a bit bigger than the car it's towing. It seems everything is small here because of the tiny streets. It would be a nightmare if your cambelt went bust on one of these one-way streets.

I step onto my bus, finding it full of people, but I don't mind as I still get to watch out the window as we move. The landscape is flat, like someone has used a rolling pin to flatten it neatly, and I think there are mountains far away but it's misty so I can't see. Forty minutes later, we are in Carmona.

Getting off, I notice a big, green cylindrical tree looking like it's covered in notes attached with string. I will come back and look at that later in more detail. I also meet the tiniest, scabbiest cat I have ever seen and talk to him but don't go near as he's all matted and dirty. He has such a sad look. I would give him a home if I lived here. Someone has kindly left a big pile of rice out for him though. He's not thin, just scabby and scared, and needs some love.

Even though it's freezing cold today and I need my gloves, I immediately like Carmona, where a big building dominates the town and walk beneath a tall archway through a huge, deep old fortress-styled wall.

I find my accommodation easily on a small white, pedestrianised street just off the plaza, which has a plaque on the wall saying Casa de Oración Madre de Dios. I ring the intercom and tell them in Spanish that I have a reservation. A nun opens the door.

She only speaks Spanish which is good and bad, getting her smartphone out from the pocket of her robe, and rings someone. It's very peaceful here, the air feels calm and there's hardly a sound.

I see a sign that says habitaciónes so I am in the right place. An inviting courtyard enclosed with glass is on the other side of a corridor, featuring brick columns, a terracotta tiled floor, and some green plants. Everything is white, soft and clean looking.

Someone else arrives who also only speaks Spanish but I manage to communicate, pleased that I know more than I realise. I give her my telephone number in Spanish, and my passport. She asks for cash and it's a good job that I have enough as places usually ask for card payment these days. The nun is lovely. I ask her if there is a kitchen to use and she says no.

We get the lift to the third floor and she talks the whole way. I am struggling to understand. She may have been given the impression that I speak Spanish when I don't. She keeps saying big and small room, and touching the key rings she is carrying. When we get to a room that looks like it's occupied, I finally understand. She wanted me to have a big room rather than a smaller one. She takes me to a small room and asks if it's OK. I say yes, I am only small, and she laughs a real belly laugh. I can't believe I made a nun laugh while talking Spanish. That's probably the first and last time that will happen.

The room is perfect with a single bed, and isn't that small. I have my own bathroom. It's basic, a tiled floor and a window with a shutter. It is cold though and I don't see any heating. I realise, too, that there is no kettle.

I hear the cleaner outside and ask her for hot water for my tea, my flask in my hand. She takes me downstairs and tries to give me directions but that's not working, so she comes with me and explains to a nun in the kitchen that I want hot water, and she puts the kettle on. This nun talks to me and I manage to chat back, finding the words to ask her if I can look around and she kindly takes me on a mini-tour, and when I speak the correct Spanish she says, 'Bueno.'

We walk around the central courtyard to a conference room and three different chapels. Two are just rooms with an altar and minimum decoration while the third is a gorgeous church with nuns inside praying. I feel like a spare part as I obviously have no faith, however I have enjoyed the tour as we get back to the kitchen. The kettle has boiled by now so I pour hot water onto my tea leaves and go back to the room.

After a small rest, I go off to explore Carmona. I need to move and warm up, I can't feel my fingers. This building is incredibly cold.

I wasn't going to visit any buildings here but the tourist information place is located near the huge wall that I walked through, which is unsurprisingly a fort called Alcázar de la Puerta de Sevilla. The woman at the desk gives me a map and explains the area. This fort is €2.00 to visit and I discover it's amazing. You walk up the stairs and the leaflet, a self-guided tour, explains where you are, along with other important information. This fort used to protect the town and its history goes back to the 8th century BC. I had no idea when I booked Carmona that it had so much history and that it's such an important place perched on the top of a hill, in such a great position for defence. If you enjoy history, then Carmona has heaps of it.

A steep climb to the top gives the most amazing 360-degree views of the town and its surroundings, while plaques tell you what all the points of interest are. I spend some time up there looking at my map, working out where I am, realising I can see the convent and its bell tower.

Reluctantly, it's time to go back down and wander slowly, there's no hurry, until I step off the small street into a huge open-air courtyard with big, white arches all the way round. Surrounding me is the best smell, so I walk towards it, finding a tapas bar in the corner with really good prices. I take a seat. Everything is in Spanish and the food is unusual so I have to translate a lot. I order two tapas and a glass of wine.

By now, with all that walking, it's boiling hot so I take my coat, cardigan, and gloves off, swapping them for my sunglasses. I could sit in the shade but don't because it's the 27th of December and I want to feel the heat on my skin. The waiter brings me a glass of white wine, so I'm pleased I got that right in Spanish and, oh my, it's delicious. I love it when a glass of wine hits the spot.

Everyone around me is drinking alcohol, the sun is burning, and I have the wrong clothes on. How could life change so fast?

I love it here, the tapas bar, and Carmona, the town. The food tastes as good as it smells. I've ordered another spinach and chickpea like I had in Seville, but this is better and comes with a sweet potato and tomato thing. Both are good sized portions, hot and full of flavour. I will be back here. When I ordered it all initially, I nearly got three items so I am glad that I didn't because this is enough and the wine just finishes it off.

I enjoy people watching, as most of us do. Two young couples in their late twenties sit not too far away and beside them is a pram with a new born inside. The couples share plates of tapas. One of the men divides something that looks like a lasagne into four pieces and they all have a mouthful. What a lovely way to spend an afternoon. The baby is sleeping too which is lucky. I never did that with any of my new born babies; we had no money, not many friends to socialise with, very few sunny afternoons, and no tapas bars to share food in.

I often wonder what it would have been like to raise children in this kind of environment. The casual outdoor eating all year round. We just don't do that in England, it's usually raining. And so we don't build up friendships like this, the kind that you would share a tapas with. I bet their mental health is better here as well. The sunshine and social circles must really help.

I head back to the convent but first stop in a round plaza, the Plaza de San Fernando, full of benches all facing in towards a Christmas tree in the middle. It's green but a cylinder again, not a tree. Handmade cards from children cover it too, which is sweet. I sit on a bench as others are doing and enjoy this weather. One man is lying down asleep on the bench, and why not?

It's a great place to just chill, meet a friend, look at the restaurants, the coming and goings, the trees, read a book, and people watch.

I get my flask out, thankful it's just warm enough. I brought a cheap charity shop flask with me and have left my best one at home in case I dented it or it got lost. It doesn't hold the heat that well but it's very welcome in this sunny spot.

When I return to the convent, the lovely nun has her hands inside her cape saying frio. It is cold, the buildings here are close together, and the alleyways don't get any sun. But I am so tired I can't stay out any longer. Upstairs, my room is so cold that I get all the blankets out and put them on my bed, lay down and fall asleep which is unlike me.

I wake up at about 5.00 pm. and eat the rest of the crisps I bought ages ago, afterwards wanting another cup of tea but not really that keen to leave my room and find someone.

I spot an air conditioner unit on the wall and turn it on, fiddling with the buttons until warmth comes out. Hooray.

Thinking about it, I should probably book a bus to Córdoba, so I search and search but find that all the sites say that there aren't any buses out of Carmona. I don't understand, I got off a bus going to Córdoba, so I was expecting to get the 10.10 am. onwards. But there aren't any buses for that time on Friday the 29th.

Oh, no.

I look for the nearest train station, finding it's Brenes – seven kilometres away – only I can't catch a bus to it from Carmona.

Oh dear, I am stuck. I have accommodation booked in Córdoba for Friday, but no buses are going to Córdoba at all until Monday. There are no buses going to Seville in the morning either. There is only a bus each evening at 8.02 pm.

I could catch that bus tomorrow and leave my bag here all day because I will still have the room, but then I wouldn't be using the second night's sleep I've already paid for, and would need to buy more accommodation in Seville, plus I like it here.

So let me think.

My accommodation in Córdoba can be cancelled until 12.00 pm., that's six hours away, so I could move the date forward and stay here. Let's do that.

But, wait, there are no buses to Córdoba from here on Saturday so that's not going to solve anything either. No buses at all to Córdoba. It seems I have no choice but to go back to Seville. I can't find any trains from that random train station to get there or I could have gotten a taxi.

This is going to cost me as I have messed up. I just need to decide what to do, but I can't think straight at the moment.

Knowing I don't want to drag my suitcase about all day, I book the bus for tomorrow while it's still available.

This is all such a shame as I wanted to spend two nights here unwinding after hectic Seville and then move on to Córdoba. How could an easy plan go so wrong?

As I check the timetables, it says the bus will get into Seville station at 8.35 pm. and the train to Córdoba is at 9.36 pm., reaching its destination at 10.34 pm. That's doable. Let's see where the train station is. According to Google, it's a 42-minute walk through the middle of Seville which will be full of people. What if I take a wrong turn down the tiny streets? I could get a taxi but then I'd have to walk half an hour to find my accommodation in Córdoba.

Gosh, I don't know what to do.

My instinct is not to wander around in Seville or Córdoba with a suitcase in the dark, so I need to stay in Seville again which is not what I planned to do.

I don't regret coming to Carmona, it's gorgeous, but I didn't expect to get stuck here. I have been lax about booking tickets on this trip; when I interrailed I usually just turned up at a station and bought one.

This is holiday time though, spanning Christmas and New Year and, in such a tiny place with no train station, I shouldn't have assumed I would get a ticket. When I booked my bus ticket here, I should have booked one out straight away as I knew the dates.

A hostel will be OK in Seville for one night. The prices start at €11, then €14, but they all look like noisy, busy young people hostels.

I could get a room for €29 with a shared bathroom. At least it will be my own space. Is the difference of €15 anything to worry about in the big scheme of things? I have spent a fortune already but I keep looking until I spot a hostel for €20 with great reviews and bunk beds with privacy curtains. Gosh, am I doing dorms again? The thought is crazy but it looks nice. And of course I can share rooms, that's all I did on my Camino for 36 days.

I won't plan on going out in the evening. I'll only want to sleep and catch a train to Córdoba the next morning. It will be fine.

Now I need to book a train for Friday morning to Córdoba, easily done.

So much for a relaxing evening, I have spent hours on the internet but it's all OK. At least it's all sorted and only cost €25 to put right, this could have been much worse.

I practise my Spanish on Duolingo for a bit. I would love a cup of tea but I am not going wandering.

It's quiet here tonight, except for the lift and the doors, and the hollow corridors where the footsteps sound loud on the tiles. At nine o'clock, I fall asleep.

Thursday 28th December

I slept for 11 hours and feel much better for it. I didn't want to run up a huge bill by leaving the heating on all night even though it was cold, but as soon as I woke up I switched it straight back on, then used the rustic shower, the kind where you have to hold the shower head.

What makes me laugh is that the shower cubicle is tiny. My head almost reaches the top of the curtains which has never happened to me before. Anyone over 5'5" would probably see over the top. Saying that, the nuns who showed me to my room were tiny, and made me feel tall, and the more I think about it, most of the nuns I have seen over the years have always been small.

I am lucky I got here so early yesterday to have a good look around and do a few touristy things. From my window, the sun looks nice today but, I imagine, misleading. It's probably cold out there too.

I would love a cup of tea but pack instead. Before I leave later, I want to stroll and get some more tapas from the same place as yesterday, knowing it will save time if I google what's on the menu.

Suddenly, the bell at the front door rings. Like I found out when I got here, you can't get in until a nun answers the big front door. Grabbing my flask, I go in search of hot water and meet a nun who waves me a kiss. How cute. I ask for hot water but she doesn't understand, however, the maid who helped yesterday is here so explains and takes the flask off me. In the meantime, the nun gives me a Spanish lesson and tells me the name of her cape which I have already forgotten. She tries to teach me new words too, being very persistent, and says I am learning so seems very pleased. She is lovely, if not a bit intense. My flask is brought back and the nun I've been chatting with touches my head, saying something else I don't understand.

It's so welcoming here that I don't want to leave. But to be honest, I am only here till 7.00 pm. and if I were staying like I'd planned, I would only be in my room after that anyway. Ready to relax a bit more before going back to a busy hotel in Seville, I drink my tea and eat a couple of biscuits and a banana for breakfast.

You have to laugh though, something is dragging me back to Seville.

After breakfast and more relaxation, I decide to visit the posh gold church here at the convent that had a couple of nuns in it when I arrived, only I wasn't sure then if I was allowed in.

Inside, I find a bench and chill but it's not long before I get restless, wanting to scroll on my phone or read something. When I booked the convent, I dreamed of sitting here, feeling at peace and calm after all that buzz, and yet now I am, I don't know what to do. I try to meditate, closing my eyes, but it's been so long that I can't get in the zone easily, so I keep trying to empty my head. This entire trip has been a whirlwind so far and an hour in here would be good for me, I think, sitting in this big, cold stone room on a wooden bench.

I open my eyes and realise I have already been here for 39 minutes. That went quickly.

Not ready to quite give up, however, I close my eyes again and hear a nun come in to sit a few rows behind me. It feels different with her here as well. This is what she does day in, day out, and I have entered her world.

I don't feel judged, she might be pleased to see me in here

using the 'facilities'. Background noises interrupt the quiet of the room, chairs being scraped on tiles somewhere, and the huge front door opening somewhere behind me.

I wonder what the nun is doing with her time. I don't want to turn and look. Is she praying or meditating? I have not given much thought to praying. I hear people say they will pray for you when times are bad or if someone is poorly but, outside of that, what is praying? There are prayers before bed which I don't do, but I think you say thanks for the day, the food, the good things, and ask for help for those who need it.

What would a nun be praying about? Especially if she comes in here a few times a day. Are prayers just about asking for help for others, the world, and peace?

I try to pray in my head, thankful for my trip, my children and my health. It all seems very self-centred.

Somewhere nearby, I hear a man singing. Come to think of it, I did hear a man's voice yesterday which felt strange in a convent. Now he is singing a lovely hymn, a nun singing along with him. I can't see the context, where they are, but it's very soothing while I am here chilling.

I try to just be at peace and let something happen.

The only thing that I want to ask for myself, if this is the place to ask, is to lose my worry. It's almost deliberating. I worry out of proportion to everyone else, as far as I know.

Before I came away on this trip, I was worried about my son visiting me in Cornwall. I almost tried to put him off to save me from worrying about him driving. What if he had a car accident? What might happen then? It would be my fault as he was driving to me. But why would it be my fault? I know it wouldn't be, it would be an accident. Someone not concentrating, the sun in his eyes, the rain. Besides, I am not the only person he sees when he comes to Cornwall so of course I shouldn't take the blame for something like that. But it feels like I should, in my heart, not in my head.

Ciara has travelled to Peru on her own, which is a worry as the country can be a little unstable. She is staying with a friend that I have met, but it's still Peru so that's a worry. I worry about Aidan and Thea too, for no reason at all, whether their jobs are safe, if they have enough money. I worry about Jamie as well, my extra son, is he OK? I should see him more. I worry about all my children every day. I can't help it, it's exhausting.

Then I have a light bulb moment. When I was about ten years old, a school friend walked to my house every day and we would go to school together, my house being right opposite.

One morning, however, she got run over on her way to my house and broke her leg. It was quite a big event in my life, it was talked about in assembly, and a lollipop lady was installed to help us all cross the road. I felt so bad seeing her leg in plaster. Back then in the 70's, plasters were huge, heavy casts. Seeing her in pain, broken, made me feel so guilty. I think her parents said it was my fault, I am not 100% sure, but I remember their faces when I visited her house. It's possible they were just upset for their daughter, although I have a feeling I wasn't welcome after that. But memories can play tricks on you.

I have been carrying that around my whole life, and yet I had forgotten it. Maybe they didn't blame me but my memory feels it all the same. Perhaps this is why I worry so much?

Maybe, now I have found the source of my worry, I can process it. I am not sure how it works. If I have felt, since I was ten years old, that it's my fault if people hurt themselves on their way to my house, then it's no wonder I worry about everything else in life.

Gosh, that's a lot to process but it does make sense.

After an hour, I leave, pleased over achieving something I wanted to do. Unwinding in this church has brought a few unexpected things to the surface I will need to work through.

Outside in the corridor, I find a wicker chair that wraps around the pretty courtyard where the nun I spoke to this morning is showing two people around. When she sees me, she stops and introduces us, giving me another Spanish lesson, so I ask where they are from because I can do that confidently. They are from Galicia. Scrambling my brain into action, I try to explain, very badly, that I walked the Camino last year. They are probably horrified at my Spanish but I manage to communicate what I want to say, and they look impressed on learning that I started in France and walked 500 miles. Happy with my new words I've learned from our conversation, we say goodbye and I know now that I need to learn some past tenses too, so I can have proper conversations in the future.

It's time to go out and the weather looks brighter. Sunglasses and gloves weather again.

I make my way over to where the bus dropped me yesterday and check out where I need to be later. It's a short walk from the convent to here, only ten minutes. Already, 16 people are waiting at the bus stop, where could they be going? I take a look at the timetable, relieved there are many buses to Córdoba and Seville.

Hmm …

Did I make a big mistake in haste by feeling under pressure yesterday? I could have come and had a look at these timetables last night but I was tired, plus there are codes next to everything which I can't understand.

Not far away, there is a resting area in the shape of a big rectangle with seats and a play area, the green cylindrical tree that I saw when I first arrived here standing proudly, so I sit down. This one-way road leads all the way round the square, so the bus stop is for both directions.

Maybe I panicked last night and shouldn't have.

When the bus arrives, it's almost empty, a bendy bus. Why didn't I know about this? I caught a really early bus here yesterday, gulping my breakfast down at the hotel when I could have been more leisurely.

As all 16 people get on, I go over and have a look. Some seem to have a card all the same colour, maybe it's a locals pass. People of all ages are on here and I think it's a local bus. I need to find out how to access that. I didn't see it online.

But it's done now. I am leaving at 8.00 pm. and I have a train to Córdoba tomorrow. It's OK. I just wish I had known, as going back to Seville wasn't part of the plan.

Once the bus drives away, I head off to find the place I ate at yesterday; it's just as sunny now. I ask for lemonade and understand when the lady there says she doesn't have any, so I order orange. I order two different tapas.

In five and a half hours, my bus will arrive. At 2.30 pm. I only have a walk planned after this which will take half an hour or maybe more, so for now I chill.

I find it difficult doing nothing though. Like when I was in the church, I want to pick up my phone and scroll, but I realise that is just a habit. What did we used to do before we had phones?

It's important to stop and live in the moment. Not constantly scan your phone for what happened yesterday, who's doing what today and who might be doing wonderful things tomorrow. Live life right now. Just stop and look around, take it all in, have a think about things. It's not easy when we are programmed to pick up our phones.

My mind tries to focus but, even now, I can't help thinking about my friend's broken leg; it makes total sense that I would carry that around with me, if that's how I felt and nobody told me otherwise. From today onwards, I need to try and remember that what happens in the world is not always my fault. I will keep reminding myself this and hope it settles.

The food here is very good. When they bring my tapas out, I try some soft, flavoured layered thing, like lasagne but there's no beef, and there are lots more layers. I think it's aubergine, very different to anything that I have had before, and the second one is a croquette with a bit of ham. The few chips are actually hot, unlike all the other chips I have had so far this trip.

After my lunch, I go to the Alcázar to admire the views as I love a visit to an historic castle. It's complicated getting up the hill – the houses are so close together with tiny lanes that weave around corners, but really you are either going up or down, so I keep climbing. Once I get to the top, I take a look at the prices to get in, only to realise it's actually a hotel, not an alcázar at all. I go in anyway. I know now that you can just wander into hotels and have a drink; maybe I will have a glass of wine here. From inside, the views are stunning, the best tables near the windows taken. However, none of this is as impressive as the hotel in Seville. Look at me turning into a snob, four-star is not good enough anymore. But it's the wrong atmosphere and the wrong vibe so I leave, taking in the view from outside, before I stroll back down all the white lanes, past lots of front doors leading onto skinny streets to the round plaza near the convent that I sat in yesterday. The bar is busy, noisy, and I consider getting a drink but, in the end, just drink the tea from my flask I've been carrying around. I sit and enjoy the warmth of the sun, like yesterday.

At 4.00 pm. I walk back down to the fort area, where under a gazebo people are dressed as the three kings with children sitting on their laps. I think the three kings bring children gifts on the 6th of December, our equivalent to Father Christmas.

Ready to go back to the convent to charge my phone and finish packing, I bump into the lovely nun as she opens the door and it's straight in with another Spanish lesson – stairs, door, up, down. She wants to teach me more, suggesting we do that this evening so I tell her about leaving early and she looks sad. I have learnt a lot from her. To change the subject, I ask to see the lemon and orange garden and she leads me out into a different courtyard. A man has been trimming the trees nearby and a box on the floor is full of huge oranges. She tells me, 'You take one to eat as these are sweet oranges, not bitter ones.' I don't take the biggest but the smallest in the box which is still huge. Next, she introduces me to José who she insists I speak to, so I tell him he has done a great job in the garden and he smiles. She is funny and we laugh.

Following this, I have my photo taken with two of the nuns in the pretty patio area before heading back to my room to practise more Spanish on Duolingo in case I don't have time at the hostel later, or forget. When I open up Facebook on my phone, one lady on a travel page is asking why there are no buses to book in Spain, exactly the same thing as I experienced yesterday. People advise her to just turn up at the bus stop. One person suggests a different website, Alsa, and guess what, there is a bus to Córdoba tomorrow at 10.10 am. Oh dear. I did mess up. I must have been on the wrong site.

But never mind, it's all a learning curve and now I have a

new website to search for buses. As I look forward to my train journey tomorrow – I do prefer trains to buses if I have a choice, they're not so claustrophobic – I hope my hostel tonight is lovely and at least I get to see Seville again. I am trying to be positive.

Now, it's 5.15 pm., all packed and ready to go. Shall I leave now? It's going to be embarrassing leaving and my new friend is going to give me another lesson if I bump into her. Maybe I will write a note and leave it for her.

With two and a half hours before my bus is due, if I leave now I'll have to take my suitcase. It's not that huge, only there will be a lot of cobblestones to drag it over. I write a note very badly in Spanish and leave it on my bedside cabinet.

As quietly as I can, I get the lift down, carrying my case, and reach the front door without seeing anyone. I leave my key quietly on the table, press the buzzer to open the big heavy door, then literally run down the tiny white street and out of sight. I am not sure why I did that. I suppose I didn't want to make a fuss or have an uncomfortable interaction. When I get to the bus stop, I try to see if there's a bar within sight that I can sit in until my bus arrives but as I'm standing there one coincidentally turns up for Seville anyway. Not my bus, that's in two hours. I really did get the timetables wrong, didn't I?

I decide this can all be bus research and climb on it. Because it's a local bus, it's probably going to stop everywhere, and it costs €2.90 which is silly when I have already paid for a bus in two hours' time, but at least I am moving and can see what the difference is.

I pull up the offline Google Maps on my phone so I can see where I am. I wish I had known about this a few days ago – well, actually for the last ten years, more like. For my interrail trip, my Camino, everywhere I have ever been. It's going to be really useful.

As I thought, we are driving into all the residential areas which is nice as I get to look around. One place looks just like Carmona and I think for a moment I have gone in a big circle. But it's not, this place just has a big central area in the shape of a rectangle with seats and a tree and people milling about.

Near the front, I can see all the interactions with the bus driver, trying my best to pick up casual conversation. A group of girls get on and natter away and I hear clothes and colours and a couple of boys' names but can't understand much.

While we drive along, I think about returning to Seville, what it will be like. This bus won't drop me off at the bus station like my other bus would've. If I had known I was going to be on this bus, which I didn't even know existed, I would have gone to a different hostel. The one I booked is nearer to the station and this bus gets in from a completely different direction.

Eventually, after a fascinating explore down the many residential streets, we arrive in Seville. It's strange being back, especially at a completely different end of the city. Google says it will take 39 minutes to get to my accommodation and I walk fast, but so many people dawdling about slow me down.

By the time I reach the hostel, I have only saved half an hour, even though my bus left Carmona two hours earlier than the one I'd originally booked, but at least I saw a different side to Seville and mingled with the locals. This evening, I'll get to see Seville lit up again at night.

This hostel has a good energy, though albeit a strange name, U-sense For You, Hostel Sevilla. Two men play Spanish guitars and sing in the downstairs seating area which is a nice welcome. My bed is on the bottom bunk and does have a privacy curtain which I love, as well as somewhere I can plug my phone in, and a little light.

It's perfect.

I put my bag in the under-bed locker, secure it with my lock that I brought with me, and go back down to listen to the music. I get a glass of sangria for €1.50. And a very nice piece of chocolate cake for €1.00.

After the music stops, I go to bed. My train is not until 12.20 pm. tomorrow, so there's no great hurry.

Friday 29th December

Last night, the bed was so cosy and comfy, and I love the effect of the privacy curtain turning it into a little house. It reminds me of when I was a child building houses under the table with a sheet. It feels very cosy. Also, no one came in late and drunk last night which can happen in a hostel when you are sharing a big room with lots of other people. Often younger people who are here to enjoy Seville and not go to bed at 10.00 pm.

It would have been perfect if one man hadn't snored all night. All night long, he didn't miss a beat.

I don't have earplugs because they never stay in so, to block him out, I squeezed my finger in my ear, and even made an ear plug out of paper and held it in. Nothing worked. I did sleep in the end but lay awake a fair bit beforehand — so very frustrating!

I get up at 9.00 am. and pack, not that I really unpacked at all. With no towel left on my bed and none brought with me, I realise I can't shower until I am at the hotel later.

Making do, I enjoy a cup of tea using the kettle in the dining area, then get going and walk leisurely to the train station. My bag is so noisy on the cobbles that people look at me, unable to hear themselves talk as they pass but there's nothing I can do about it.

Three hours left to go till my train to Cordoba.

And guess what? On my way, I notice a random shop selling decorations with Feliz Navidad on them. They are not the luxury items I was looking for but, at this stage, I am going to just buy them. I grab a few bits and two more cork passport holders like the one that I bought in Setenil last week, last month, whenever it was, it's all a blur. Thinking about it though, I'm disappointed that I didn't get Ciara one when I had that first chance. I wasn't sure if she had a passport cover and I love mine, so I buy one for her anyway and for my friend, Tami. This must be the reason why I have been dragged back to Seville.

I manage to make my way to the station correctly without turning my data on by using my downloaded map, and a bit of extra knowledge by knowing roughly where I am. Eventually, a signpost turns up as I near the station and I swiftly follow other people with their own suitcases. As soon as I get there, I order a McDonald's breakfast, muffins with tomato puree, just because I want to sit down, my shoulders hurting from dragging the case over the cobbles. I have walked 7,933 steps so far today, each and every one spent dragging it behind me. No wonder my shoulder hurts.

Now I have eaten a lot of toast and tomato in Spain, this feels like a very typical breakfast, only McDonald's style, with chips and an English tea. Random, but not great. There aren't enough tomatoes and the bun is dry though the chips are a treat, plus it's a cheap experience.

The notice boards from here show all the timetables for the right buses and I wait for the 12.20 pm. to show. The board says Granada but I can't see one going to Córdoba at that time. At 12.00 pm. however, it appears so I make my way over. It's a strange system of eight long, open escalators going down to the platform but, instead of rushing down, you get your ticket scanned at the top of the escalator first. I get in the queue and check with the lady that this train is going to Córdoba before going down the slope, meeting a lot of congestion as everyone queues to have their bags scanned. I remember doing this in Santiago, it's like being at an airport. Stressful. There are so many people in this queue it doesn't feel like it will leave on time and, after that, another queue to show your ticket again. By the time I get on the train, I am shattered. I sit in the first chair I see only, moments later, a man claims it's his. Apparently, we have allocated seats. I stand up swiftly, embarrassed, then lift my case but the handle breaks as a piece of metal flies off. I can't see where it landed. Now, I am holding the handle, and the bag on the floor. I am very stressed now so I go out into the corridor to breathe. There's no way I am going searching for my allocated seat on this busy train. I put the bag back together but it's broken, the

91

bit of metal I can't find was the only thing holding it together. I might be able to manage, the cobblestones have clearly ruined it.

The train, amazingly, leaves on time. I slip back into the carriage, finding a pull-down seat next to all the luggage so I grab it, watching the scenery out the window, all flat and uninspiring. I was going to read my Kindle on this journey but I am too stressed. It's only a 40-minute journey.

I hope Córdoba is as lovely as people say and I'm looking forward to spending four nights somewhere, staying put for a bit. Tonight will be the fourth different bed in a row.

Once the train pulls up at the station, I have to brave the 25-minute walk with a dodgy bag but thankfully I make it to Hotel Maestra in one piece. I am in the old part of town again which I always enjoy.

Córdoba feels like a mini Seville but far more child friendly. There's an amusement place with rides and some of the Christmas lights hanging above the streets have cute teddy bears on them.

The hotel is OK, a reception area on one side of the courtyard, a small seating area, and a realistic Nativity scene acting as my welcome. When I check in, the receptionist gives me a map and tells me where the main attractions are. My room is near the front door so it might be a bit noisy but she says it's a big room. I don't know why everyone wants to give me a big room.

I chill and drink the tea that I made at the hostel and breathe out for half an hour, looking at my map and tucking into the crackers and a triangle of cheese I acquired at breakfast a few days ago. Before I go out and explore, I ask about a kettle and the answer is yes. Brilliant news, as I am here for four days. I put it in my room.

The hotel is right by the river and I admire the old historic bridge, heading towards the tourist office to get some more advice and a bigger map. I wander around the outside of the Mezquita, the huge mosque with incredibly tall walls that is the main attraction of Córdoba. I am not sure how to do this, perhaps I could join a guided tour? But I haven't made up my mind. I could google what to look at inside the Mezquita or find some information online, or buy a book? I haven't decided yet but I am not going inside any buildings today. I have three whole days here.

I ask the lady in the tourist information centre what is happening for the New Year here and she tells me about a party, circling where it is on the map. I will ask reception back at my hotel about that too.

Along the street, all the restaurants are overflowing with delicious smells and people eating outdoors. I look at some menu boards as I pass by but it's all confusing, full of words I don't understand.

Instead, I visit the supermarket near my hotel and buy a salad bowl, a cake, a savoury pastry, and oat milk for my proper tea bags. I haven't had a PG Tips since I left England. I also buy a bottle of fizzy orange and a carton of rosé wine for €1.15 which is probably going to be awful.

This is much better value than eating out; it feels good to get a few things in since I am staying here for a few days.

Back in my room, the salad bowl tastes good. The pasta makes it filling and I indulge in a very welcome cup of PG Tips tea with oat milk, and a little apple cake thing.

By now, it's five o'clock so I hang up my clothes in the wardrobe instead of living out of the suitcase, then scroll Facebook, just chilling for a bit, before it's time to head out for a stroll. I don't have a detailed map with street names so I just wander. Córdoba is a good size and I feel optimistic that I won't get lost. Following some Christmas lights, I end up in a square, then a road full of lights and a shopping area with a big, curved blanket of lights over my head that goes on forever down the shopping street. I admire the scale of it when some music comes on and the lights dance in tune to Spanish Christmas songs. It's a great atmosphere and reminds me of Málaga a bit. People stop to look and we all have a moment together.

I can't believe all the shops are open and everyone is out and about. It's busier than a weekday afternoon in Truro. And it's not cold but not warm either. There are just so many people and so many restaurants open, some with patio heaters.

Turning the corner, I meet the kids' area that I saw earlier, now in a blaze of colour and noise as a funfair where you can buy a set of tickets to go on whatever you like, there's so much choice. What a treat. There's even a small ice rink. The place is alive, definitely family-friendly. I would love to have brought my children here when they were small.

With the night coming to an end, I find my way back to the hotel, quite pleased with myself. I even have a glass of wine from my €1.15 box – surprisingly, it's not too bad. Not great but I have tasted worse.

I book a walking tour for 11.00 am. tomorrow in hope it will give me a better idea of Córdoba, then practise my Duolingo, scroll Facebook some more, and go to sleep.

Saturday 30th December

At 8.00 am., after a good sleep, I jump out of bed and go straight out. Apparently, you can get into the Mezquita for free at 8.30 am. In my eagerness, I am a little early so stroll over the long bridge crossing the river, relishing the quiet all around me. This peaceful atmosphere is worth getting out of bed for.

When I get to the Mezquita, I count 17 people anxiously wondering if they are in the right place. By the time we're allowed to go in, there are too many to count. My excitement spills over as we're about to enter the garden area, queuing up with so many people around me; I have wanted to be here ever since I read All My Mothers. Excitement buzzes off everyone else too, already they have opened two other gates as more visitors flood in.

Me being speedy and light on my feet, I have a good position in the queue, ready to be scanned by security. The queue moves fast and I am just happy to be in it, then … wow. There is no other word, the view is overwhelming.

Columns stand in rows, arches joining them together, with vertical bold stripes alternating between stone and a rich terracotta colour. The effect of the columns and arches built up layer by layer is unusually stunning. I knew a little about the Mezquita already, having done some research, but I wasn't prepared for the scale of this. It is huge.

I almost run to the furthest point, with no idea where I am going, to move away from people. Most have stopped in awe to take photos of this unique building so early in the morning with very few visitors. We all disperse quite quickly with it being so big.

It feels like I am walking on a new morning floor that no one has touched today. I get some great photos with no one in them, then a few including people as you need them to show the scale of the place. It's vast and deep and magnificent, with a red tiled floor.

I walk about, taking a new photo with every step. All around the edges of the building are small chapels, each behind a steel gate and each with its own personality.

In the centre is a cathedral, with completely different décor. The whole layout of this building is unusual. So much history, with the mosque influences and a cathedral, all in the one building.

I do love the intricate patterns within the stone walls, similar in style to parts of the Alcázar of Seville. It's a huge space with lots to look at.

In the far corner, I take a seat on the only benches I can see and just absorb it all for a while, facing a chapel being photographed a lot by people. It's simply beautiful. The plaque says, 'Altar del Santísimo Sacramento.' Every inch of the walls, ceilings and arches is painted in soft pastel paints. It's gorgeous.

I think I will come back tomorrow and do it all again.

My phone battery is almost dead from taking loads of photos. Clearly, I didn't charge it long enough so I return to the hotel and charge it before my walking tour, taking the time to eat my orange that the nun gave me.

It's huge. I don't generally eat oranges. Actually, I never eat oranges but I want to eat this one. Like she said, this type of orange is not like the bitter ones that grow in the streets, it's sweet and has a thick skin. It's been that long since I ate one that I can't remember what to do. I ate lots when I was pregnant with Liam, six in a row one evening. Hardly any since.

However, this orange is amazing. Juicy and sweet. It also reminds me of that lovely nun. I get in a horrible mess eating it but this is the first orange I have enjoyed in almost 30 years; it's quite a moment, and one of the little things that I love about travelling. The surprises that you could not have predicted.

Drinking a cup of tea, I read my Kindle for half an hour while my phone is charging before heading out to the meeting point where the walking tour will begin in Plaza Tendillas. This is where the New Year party is going to be – I can already glimpse a stage.

Out here, it's really cold. So cold that when I sit on a marble bench I jump up at the touch. I need my hat and gloves again today, the cold reaches everywhere in the shade but it's warmer in the sunshine, at least.

While I wait for the tour group to arrive, I consider how important books are. I am only here in Córdoba because of a book that I read, All My Mothers; now I am writing about my trip and maybe it will encourage someone else to want to come here. I have always been an avid reader, less so when I had three children to raise but I got back into it. I loved reading as a child and books were always very welcome birthday gifts – Charlotte's Web, Enid Blyton stories, Helen Keller's Teacher, and all the Heidi books stood proudly on my bookshelf. I owned all three Heidi books in big hardbacks which I treasured.

Since then, my own other two books, I Hope There's a Kettle in My Room and Odd Poles and Baggy Trousers on the Camino de Santiago, have encouraged people to travel. Readers have messaged me and written lovely reviews saying that they were inspired. We are all little tourist information centres, sharing our experiences, inspiring each other.

By now, a lot of walking groups are convening in the square, including 10 of us in the English group but, as usual, there are no English people here, only me. Our guide points out a rooftop bar in the building that I took a photo of yesterday, perhaps going there while I'm here might be a possibility.

Once everybody has arrived, our guide leads us to the Jewish Quarter, explaining how some residents were allowed to build an extra one metre on their houses, the reason why the streets are so close together now and built in odd shapes; not everyone chose to extend.

After this, we step into a tiny courtyard, home to a 200-year-old orange tree. There seem to be many stories about the origins of the Seville oranges and its uses across history. Many years ago, it's thought that some illnesses made surrounding streets smell bad, and orange blossoms smell great, so people planted orange trees everywhere. These trees were thought to bring happiness to anyone who planted them. They were also used in medicine and, of course, to make marmalade for the British and, on telling this part, our guide points me out. Marmalade is delicious, I don't know why the Spanish don't eat it as much as we Brits do.

The guide goes on to show us the patios, which are really important in Córdoba. The style of the patio houses has a big emphasis on the courtyard, or patio area, going back many years, the idea being that the central courtyard was used for washing, cooking, ventilation and socialising.

A few families might share one patio and have one room upstairs to sleep in, sharing everything else.

The guide explains a bit about the Mezquita and how it has been extended over the years, how it's called the 'Mosque-Cathedral' because it has a Christian cathedral in the middle of the mosque which I feel lucky to have seen already.

We finish the tour near my hotel so I go back for a cuppa and snack, choosing to sit in the pretty patio area full of blue tiles and greenery with my tea. After a while, it gets too cold, so cold that I'm shaking, and I retreat to a comfy chair next to a piano and Belén. I am not going to re-create what I had in my Seville hotel. Here, I just wanted to be amongst people but there aren't any. Sadly, so far this has not been a very social trip.

Wanting a stroll to warm up, I search for something hot to eat as I am feeling a bit wobbly. It takes me ages to make a decision but I find somewhere very interesting, a patio in the Jewish Quarter with a tower of blue flowerpots and a very tall orange tree in the corner, climbing the same wall the flowerpots sit on. What a great setting, and the hot food will be exactly what I need. Once I've ordered, a big plate of steaming hot ratatouille with chips and two fried eggs comes out to me. Its delicious warmth is welcome and filling.

Afterwards, I cross the long bridge to see what's on the other side, which is not a great deal and it smells different on this side – they seem to have drainage issues. A plaque for Santiago makes me smile, showing Camino Mozárabe of

Santiago and its 998 kilometres. When I did my Camino, I only walked about 800 kilometres so this is much further.

Today, my app tells me I've walked 20,000 steps and it feels like it, so I return to my hotel and run a bath. Like last time, I have to make my own plug again but that's OK, I am getting good at making bath plugs. And what a lovely soak it is, there's nothing like it after a busy day.

I spend the rest of the evening looking through all the information I have about Córdoba, the paperwork the hotel gave me, tourist information suggestions and notes I have made myself from research, plus Facebook suggestions of different sites. There's a lot to do. It's all a bit overwhelming.

The problem is that tomorrow is New Year's Eve and everywhere seems to be shut. And Monday, the day after, is when the buildings usually shut, meaning I have a list of three things that I want to do on Tuesday. I am due out of the hotel on Tuesday morning, so I am hoping to stay a couple more days but haven't decided whether to stay here or go somewhere else. This is a good spot, a lovely room, at a good price and I do have a kettle. In some ways, it would be silly to move on. But I am trying to keep a tab on the purse strings so book a hostel in the Jewish Quarter which looks a bit quirky, even splashing out an extra €2.00 a night for an all-female dorm. From my experience, it's usually men who snore but that's not set in stone.

While I'm at it and seem to know what my future plans are for the following few days, I also book somewhere in Priego de Córdoba which the lady in the tourist information mentioned when I asked her for suggestions on pretty towns between here and Granada. I research Priego de Córdoba and it looks like somewhere I'd like, seeming to be a balanced mix of nature and an interesting town.

I start searching for the cheapest accommodation again and one stands out, a converted monastery with great views, plus it's in the centre. I book three nights. After that, I think I will go to Granada.

Sunday 31st December

It's the last day of 2023. I am not a morning person and I didn't want to get up, but I do love it out on Córdoba streets when it's quiet.

Off I go again to the Mezquita but I am told you need to buy a ticket because it's Sunday. Oh, never mind. It was a bit indulgent to go back inside for free. I will try on Tuesday.

My next plan after the Mezquita was to wander around the Jewish Quarter while it was still quiet. Here, being a little earlier, a lot of restaurants are obviously not open yet so the streets are much quieter than I have ever seen before. I stumble upon Calleja de las Flores, a tiny alleyway of houses, painted white with a couple of little arches and blue flowerpots on the walls. If I put my elbows out, I could probably touch both sides. It was very busy here yesterday and I snap some lovely photos, even recording a little video. The flowerpots are spilling over with greenery and red poinsettias, making the alleyway seem even smaller.

As I walk back down the tiny street, an American mum and two teenage kids are there trying to take photos. The boy suggests to his mum that maybe they should come back when the sun is brighter, as it's very grey right now. As they are English speaking, I point out it will be really busy with people later and she says to me, 'It's not much, is it?', obviously meaning the place in general. I am disappointed for her. This street is so pretty, a real little gem, but Instagram probably blew it out of proportion and she expected more, whereas I stumbled across it yesterday and have loved my walk up and down the tiny street. It's really cute.

After I have enough photos, I explore Los Patios de San Basilio which I haven't been to yet as it's a few minutes' walk away in an area of its own, and admire the lovely, long regimented streets with cobbled floors, with no cars driving through. The three streets are all parallel with each other, very organised housing compared to the Jewish Quarter, but I can't find the Basilio with the five patios that the lady on reception pointed out.

I do come across a stunning piece of art made up of two statues: an elderly man on the ground and a child up a ladder. They are cast in bronze, emanating so much detail from the intent look on the old man's face as he passes up a flowerpot to the child on the ladder. It all feels so real, as if he is really standing there. The whole thing is life-sized, the child on the ladder reaching down to take the pot from his grandad, beautiful. You can see the chemistry between the two of them, the look in their eyes, the details of their clothes. On the wall sit the blue patio pots with flowers spilling out, one flowerpot in the man's hands. I feel like they are both here, and not statues at all. It has captured the essence of Córdoba, the patios and flowers. I love it.

Round and round I go, up and down the streets, trying to find the starting point to Los Patios de San Basilio until the penny drops. I keep seeing patio plaques on people's walls and some are numbered, so you must have to buy a ticket to get into these individual patios. I thought coming here would be visiting a building that then had patios, looking forward to getting out of the cold. But it clearly doesn't work like that.

I think access into the patios begins at 10.30 am. or at least you can buy your tickets then. Right now, it's only 9.45 am. so I go back to the hotel; it's too cold to sit on a park bench for that long. Plus, I need a cup of tea.

Already quite tired despite a good sleep, I see that I have walked 7,000 steps; I should probably try and get a nap this afternoon ready for New Year's Eve.

Checking my phone, Phil has messaged me, saying he's off to Plymouth for his New Year's Eve party where we went last year. I would love to be joining him as it was a lot of fun last year, and the year before. It's sad to think he's going on his own, although he's OK with that and we have friends there he can sit with. But still, it does feel very selfish today, choosing to be here and not at home.

But you can't have everything. I might have chosen to do this but it doesn't mean that I won't miss him.

Once I'm feeling refreshed, I go back out to the patios and buy a ticket. It feels wrong walking into someone's house and garden just to gawp but that's what I have paid to do, and they seem happy enough to let me in.

At one patio, an elderly man quietly greets me, where it's just the two of us standing there. You don't look around the house, just admire the flowers, and it feels a little wrong. I ask him in Spanish if he lives here, and for how long. He replies that he has lived here his whole life and looks so proud, it's really sweet.

The next patio has a detailed Nativity scene, again with a man welcoming me in, but also some wooden models of his patio and another one very similar to a doll's house with no roof, so you can see down onto the scenes from above. These models are so clever, obviously made with a lot of enthusiasm and love.

The patio after that, the man standing there shows me a photo of what it looks like in summer in full bloom, every space on the walls bursting with colour. There's a lovely vibe to the whole thing and it makes me envious to have a patio of my own, but of course it would be wet all the time.

When I have finished exploring the patios, I pop into a café advertising toast and coffee for €2.00, finding it very Spanish and spacious inside, with four men are sitting at the back playing a game on the table, possibly dominoes. I get my tea and the bread is fresh and warm, though there's not enough tomato on my toast and soon my tiny cup of tea is nearly all gone. Do I have the guts to go ask for more? Yes, I do, but I take a handful of coins. It's so cheap in here that I don't want to eat into their profits but I would enjoy my toast with more tomato and a top-up of water. The man behind the till doesn't speak English but that's OK as I'm managing now with the basics, so drop 50 cents on the counter, putting my cup down, and ask for more hot water and another tomato sachet. He takes the 50 cents, and I sit back down to enjoy my tea and toast, working out where to go next.

I want to try and find the Belén in the central area. On my way, after I'm done in the café, I pop into a supermarket and get a box of three Cup a Soups.

As I near the place with the Belén, a church door is open and a service is on, so I move away fast. I am not getting involved with that again. Soon, however, I come to another church with a sign outside saying Belén Centro Cultural San Hipólito. I step inside.

Wow, it's gorgeous. I am really enjoying these visits. I wish now that I had gotten in that long queue in Seville and seen the one there but I wasn't as obsessed with them back then as I am now.

Here, a model of the Nativity scene is about 10 feet wide, and deep as well. With trees, mud houses, a muddy floor, people, animals pulling carts, chickens, sheep, a lady making bread, a camel carrying baskets, and even a camel lying on the ground, I just love the whole feel of it. As I am not religious, the actual crib scene doesn't affect me but I can picture living there, being inside this scene with the mud under my feet.

They even dim the light, so you can see it at night-time. It's astonishing. I admire it for a long time.

My map tells me there are three more churches nearby, so off I go in search of them, finding the doors of the first one are shut but the second, a beautiful white church, is open.

I wander about leisurely before deciding to go back. As I pass a tempting churros stall, I saw them in Málaga, Ronda and Seville and didn't buy any, so I decide that now is the time to get some. Since I arrived, there has always been a queue for this stall but only one family is in front of me now. I have never bought churros before and I'm not quite sure what to do. The girl at the stall doesn't speak English at all so I struggle to order. A huge donut circle comes out of the fryer and she snips it with scissors.

I walk away holding a large cone of three pieces of crunchy fried dough and a pot of chocolate, then head back to my room, only two minutes away. Once there, I make a cup of tea, sit on my bed, and eat the churros. The chocolate liquid is a bit thin and, by the time I eat the third churro, I am feeling a bit sick. I might not eat them again, I think this was a one off. But I think I enjoyed it.

Checking my app again, I see that I have walked 18,000 steps so far and it's only almost three o'clock; no wonder I am shattered. Time for a nap before New Year.

I sleep for two hours and wake up feeling really groggy.

Boiling the kettle, I make a Cup a Soup to wake up properly, open my tin of puy lentils and tip half into the soup before pouring it into my flask as I don't have anything else here to use. My plastic spoon that came with my churros comes in handy to stir it with and I take a sip. Delicious. I will do more of this. It's cost-effective and I know what I am getting.

Not quite ready to go out again, I read The Red House by Roz Watkins – a proper page turner – on my Kindle, wanting to stay here in my hotel room in the warmth. When I knew I would be away for New Year, I thought I would be indoors because that's how I always picture New Year, not outdoors all evening. We can't do that in England. Tonight, I will put an extra layer on and won't take a bag, just my waist belt for phone, key and money. I might even wear two pairs of leggings as it's going to be nippy and I obviously want to stay out till 12.00 am.

Eventually, after pulling myself away from my room, I find my way to Plaza de las Tendillas to check where the stage will be set up for later on, only to find it all dark where nothing is happening with barely any people. I walk along the street, José Cruz Conde, and find that, there too, it's eerily quiet.

Everything is shut – such a huge contrast to the other day when it was filled with prams and families going in and out of shops.

The sheet of lights is on and, as I walk by, they burst into life with music and dancing. I stop and watch along with a few others but it's a huge depletion of people compared to the other day. I don't know what to do. A few bars are scattered about, overspilling with people, mostly youngsters. Where are all the families and people my age?

Nearby, a few well-dressed people walk past with New Year's Eve clothes on, women well turned out and men with heavy stylish winter coats. Some are carrying little bags, maybe gifts, some even seem to have cake. I glimpse a pie large enough to feed a huge family and some people carry boxes that look like panettone, only much bigger than I have ever seen. Perhaps they are going to family gatherings or to hotel do's?

I sit down in the square with the stage set up where there's a strong police presence. Again, the marble bench is so cold that I can't sit on it for too long until an English lady comes over and asks if I know what's going on. How does she know I am English?

I say that I thought everything was happening here where the stage is. She goes and asks the police and they say it is here, that you need to get here early as it will be busy. But it is early and nothing is happening. You think there would be music of some sort as they have already put the stage up. Perhaps everyone is still eating?

I move on to the big square, Plaza de la Corredera, but it's empty, there are no lights and no people. It only seems huge and vast with nobody here. A man wheeling the last of his chairs from an eatery is trawling them all back inside while, meanwhile, I notice there's just one bar open, again overflowing with younger people.

After wandering about, I arrive at the Mezquita, looking lovely with its huge walls lit up. The streets are empty here too. I go onto the bridge and take a few night-time photos, taking the route alongside the river back towards my hotel, but walk past and back up the hill. The smell of chips cooking from a busy kebab shop wafts my way, making me really want some. A long queue spills out onto the street from its doors and I browse the packed menu, unable to believe I am even looking at it, but I am very hungry. Besides, nothing else seems to be open.

I join the queue before quickly changing my mind, heading back up to Tendillas instead, only at the top of this road. It's slightly busier but not by much.

However, the kebab shop calls me back, partly because of my hunger and partly because I don't know what else to do with my spare time. I join the long queue again but there's no hurry. It might be chaos here, so busy that they haven't managed to clean the tables yet, but at least it's full of people.

It's funny. What am I doing in a kebab queue on New Year's Eve in Spain? It doesn't feel real. Before I know it, I have ordered number four, a meal deal of a chicken burger, chips and an orange Kas. I get given a plastic disc with 19 on it and sit at a dirty table to wait. This wasn't how I pictured my New Year's Eve. I feel bad that I ordered chicken too, being mostly vegetarian or vegan when I can, but I have no willpower when I am hungry.

After a while, the man behind the till calls out, 'Diecinueve.' That's me.

And so I walk back up to the square carrying my plastic bag full of food. Music plays now, although it's a bit lame. I sit on a cold marble bench and eat my dinner.

The chips are covered in a white sauce, mayo of some sort which I wasn't expecting, and a red one. It is warm and filling and immediately gives me that heavy greasy feeling. There are a few people here now. A lady stands next to me and opens her carrier bag to reveal a bottle of fizz and a small plastic container with grapes neatly arranged in a circle. So the grapes are a thing here? I didn't look into that and I don't have any Wi-Fi to look them up now.

When I've finished eating, I get up because my bum is so cold and throw away the packaging into a nearby bin. There are still a lot of police around the square, including five brightly coloured ambulances who have joined them, but we still have a long wait to go before the night really begins. All around, English music plays which disappoints me as I wanted something Spanish while I was in Spain, the song Saturday Night (Be my Baby) encouraging people to dance.

Strangely, I feel a bit detached. This really isn't my thing but what can I do now? I am feeling a bit lonely.

Phil is in Plymouth at his own New Year's Eve do and, to be perfectly honest, I would rather be there with him. Not rather be at home – I am enjoying my trip – but right now, in this exact moment, that's where I would rather be.

I walk over to the blanket of lights and sit on one of the

many wooden things holding the lights up. Being small, it's a bit far off the ground for me but at least I manage to climb up. The wood is warmer than the marble.

More tragic disco music plays and yet I am surrounded by orange trees. I wonder what the new year will bring. The year of 2023 has been a mixed year. I moved out of Phil's which was difficult but we hope to move back in together at some point. It's the village where we lived that didn't suit me, so I am back in my own town with my friends and family, and it's only a ten-minute drive to work and within walking distance to the sea. I don't need a new year to create a long to-do list. I am doing what I love, right now.

I have a good job, maybe not financially, but I love my workplace and work colleagues. It's flexible and the money I earn lets me do this. I don't spend money on much else.

At 10.55 pm., we only have one hour to go, though I am getting cold sitting still so I move again.

Cotton Eye Joe plays next, it's all very random, like a naff wedding.

I make my way into the centre of the square which is filling up now and lean on a black structure, finding it's the snow machine blowing tiny bits of biodegradable paper every so often to keep the children amused.

People are wearing silly hats and flashing ears and funny glasses. It's all a bit predictable now that I understand what it is, yet quite reassuring to think that the Spanish can't do any better than England at these kinds of events. Especially with the English music.

Oh dear, a trigger song plays next. Breathe.

I try to face it. Once, I was in Asda when a trigger song from my past came on and I walked out, then a second time, I tried to work through it. I am going to do that now because I don't want to leave. It's just a song, only three minutes long, and it's my attitude to it that counts. I need to remember how far I have come. But it does remind me of intense emotional times. My marriage is condensed into this song, all 19 years into three minutes. Whooshes of good, bad and very ugly.

But it's over. I did it.

And I am not letting my mind drift off, I need to pull it back. I am getting far better at it now. I find songs can trigger memories that your brain attaches itself to and then wanders off. You know you don't want to go there, but you can't control it. I am learning to get some of that control back. It feels like my memories are inside one of those tubes you slide down at a swimming pool, twisting and turning, only my tunnel is not brightly coloured, it's black. It's so easy to slip down the slide and end up somewhere mentally that I don't want to go. Instead, I picture a huge, solid manhole cover, heaving it across to cover the hole. While I am covering it, I am peeping down the hole and can see the memories, black and ugly, but I get the cover across, albeit slowly, and I am OK.

I bring myself back to the square, look around at where I am, feel the energy and the people and shut off that part of my brain. It will only take a few minutes as I am getting better at it.

With only 50 minutes to go, I suddenly feel I should probably go back to the hotel, that these situations are not for solo people. There are families here, drunk people, happy people. It's not for a strange, cold, 58-year-old woman from England with four tops on, two trousers, a hat, gloves and a loud flowery raincoat. I don't look the part and I don't feel it.

Like a Virgin by Madonna plays now which is OK, she has some good songs. Then three drunk-looking men nearly crash into me, squashing me against the snow machine. They keep staring at me and I feel vulnerable as it's obvious I am on my own. They are drinking out of wine cartons like the one I have in my room, but they have two each. They will have no stomach linings left if they drink all that; it's not expensive to get drunk here if you have no taste buds. I move away from the centre as I don't feel comfortable anymore.

Looking around, everyone has carrier bags with drinks in them. A cheap night out, I suppose, as there's no bar you can bring your own. There's lots of random dancing going on from different people and it's chillier here, while it was warmer in the middle bit. Someone comes out onto the stage but I can't understand them. The drunks are still in my spot, so I walk around the square. Billy Jean plays now, what a strange playlist – the best and worst of British music.

It takes me four minutes to do a lap of the square, bringing the time to 11.25 pm. That means I have 35 minutes left. Divide that by four and I have about eight laps to go.

There are lots of exits off the square and I count five police cars, three vans and a fire engine truck. I don't like being in places where it's so volatile but there are only 30 minutes to go now. The laps become harder as so many people keep arriving, floods of them now, complete with prams and buggies and cold babies, and another fire extinguisher truck to add to the mix. What on earth might happen here?

One policeman looks at me funny, and I realise my behaviour must look a bit suspicious, so I stop walking and move into the packed huddle. It's a great atmosphere now more people are here, some standing on balconies from the hotel and the rooftops.

Finally, there are just a few minutes left until midnight. Two people are on stage talking and then a countdown begins – five, four, three, two, one! – and it all goes surprisingly quiet. This is not how we celebrate New Year in England, we scream and shout and run around kissing everyone, then cross arms and sing Auld Lang Syne.

A little bit of instrumental music plays, however, and everyone is waiting. Then a ping, like a guitar chord, sounds out and everyone pops a grape in their mouths, then another ping and another grape, and another. One grape to each ping of music.

It's bizarre. They are counting, eight, nine, but because they have a mouth full of grapes, it's not very clear.

Then lots of noise and fireworks go off over my head which I wasn't expecting – that explains the fire trucks. Everyone is still munching on their grapes while admiring the firework display, which is quite impressive. It's not a long show and it's all over in five minutes as a band comes out onto the stage to start performing live. They might be singing Time Warp in Spanish, I am not sure, but it's definitely time for me to leave. Despite all its eccentricities, I have enjoyed tonight and I'm glad I stayed out to take part.

On my way back to the hotel, I stop in a shop to buy a small can of cider and a bag of those nut and corn things, before settling down on my bed to enjoy it all. I have loads of messages on my phone now that I am back in Wi-Fi range. Phil's had a great time and sent me a video of the dancing and our friends waving hello at me.

It looks like Aidan and Thea are having fun too. Ciara hasn't gone out yet to celebrate but she's five hours behind in Peru.

Well, that's it for the new year.

I have walked 31,807 steps today. Oh my.

Monday 1st January 2024

I wake up with a sore throat, not feeling great. Without any throat lozenges, I drink lots of green tea to ease the pain instead. Maybe over 30,000 steps yesterday was too much.

I don't feel well enough to go anywhere and, besides, I think everything is shut today anyway. I finish my book and write a praising review on Amazon, then scroll Facebook for a bit before getting ready to make my Cup a Soup with lentils at around two o'clock. The kettle is in the bathroom, plugged into the shaver socket, as there's only one socket in the bedroom and no hostess corner, no cups or sugar, coffee, tea, or little plastic pots of milk, so I wait for it to boil in the small space.

While no one was looking yesterday, I picked up an orange off the ground because they are fascinating me. I picked two up in Málaga and left them behind and now I know from the walking tours that you can't eat them, but I still need to know more. The smell of these oranges hits you sometimes as you walk by the trees in the street. I would love to be here in the spring when the orange blossom is out, I must do that.

While I keep waiting for the kettle to boil, I peel one of these oranges to see how bitter they really are, just out of curiosity. How bitter is bitter?

The stolen orange peels easily enough, looking just like a proper orange. Surely it's harmless? I pop a segment in my mouth and crunch on it, before immediately spitting it out into the sink. Wow, that taste is severe, the most intense, bitter flavour I have ever experienced.

But at least I have tried it. It's nothing like marmalade, nothing at all.

A shop in Seville sold everything to do with its oranges, from chocolate and perfumed candles to soaps, but they just seem to get squashed by cars here in Córdoba. If I lived here, I would be out foraging and making something with them, probably marmalade. There must be lots that you could do with them.

Even after my lentil soup, I can still taste its bitter flavour prickled in my mouth, and my tongue feels fizzy like it's been stung with a nettle. That orange smell is so strong too. My gloves smelled of orange yesterday and it's not like I held it for very long.

By 2.30 pm., I brave a gentle stroll to get some fresh air, knowing it will turn dark soon, and plod around the neighbourhood slowly. One of the few supermarkets that are open sell ice cream so I buy some to ease my throat, as well as two oranges. It's really strange, because I never eat oranges, ever. It seems I have rediscovered them on this trip, and it's all that lovely nun's fault. My body must be craving vitamin C, but it's never asked for oranges before. Maybe it's because, since I landed in Málaga, I have seen oranges everywhere, and sublimely I now want some.

I also get a salad bowl and a banana. In the fruit section, I see the little packets of grapes that the lady in the square had yesterday, costing €1.69 for 12 grapes, all neatly arranged in a circle with a clock on the packet. They also sell them in tiny ring-pull cans. I buy a little handful from a bunch, it seems right, plus it'll be more vitamin C.

I see another nuns' convent, the same one we saw on our walking tour when they told us that this one sells sweets. Tempted, I walk up to the door but chicken out. There are no prices, just a picture of a nun stuck to an iron gate reading 'Dulces'. I retreat down the slope, then climb back up, down again, up again. I don't know what I need to do to buy the sweets … do I ring a bell? Since I don't like many types of sweets and I don't know how much they are, I would only be doing it for the novelty factor and I don't have money to waste on something I might not like, so in the end I return to the hotel.

When I open the door of my room, the smell of oranges hits me straight away. I can't believe it –I only peeled one. It's not unpleasant, I am just surprised by how very different and intense these oranges seem to be compared to the normal ones. I must come back when the blossom is out.

After two oranges and 14 grapes today, that should hopefully boost my immune system. It might not be the right amount of grapes I've eaten, or the right time of day to eat them, or even the right day at all, so I'm not sure it will bring me any luck. I eat my salad bowl now too, which I am getting a bit addicted to.

This has been a non-eventful afternoon in my hotel room but probably what I needed. With not much luck booking a bus to Priego de Córdoba, my next destination, I will visit the bus station tomorrow and talk to a human instead.

To close off the day, I start reading a new book, The Short Straw by Holly Seddon, and get an early night.

Tuesday 2nd January

When I wake up after 10 hours' sleep, I hesitantly swallow and sniff, trying to work out if I'm still ill. Luckily, I don't think I am worse than yesterday. At least that's something.

Today, however, I can't help feeling a little detached and lonely. Since I left England, I haven't had a conversation for more than three minutes with anyone. I might love my own company but this is a step too far. I miss conversation and human interaction. Plus, I am not feeling great which does bring you down a bit.

To make things worse, I had a nightmare last night, only it was me in danger this time, not my children which is what usually happens. I have almost forgotten it already though, so hopefully it won't pop up again without warning halfway through the day.

Making the most of the room, I decide to have one last bath if my DIY plug works since I am off to the hostel in a couple of hours. After so much solitude, I think a hostel is a good move.

After my bath and once I'm ready for the day, I leave at 11.00 am. even though I could've stayed till 12.00 pm. as the staff will probably want to clean the room and it's going to take extra work this morning; no one else has been here for four days. Whenever I stay in a hotel, I never like the thought of someone cleaning up my mess and making my bed every day, it seems so extravagant and unnecessary, so I always hang the Do Not Disturb sign on the doorknob. The room isn't too bad, I haven't made a mess, just a big pile of food wrappers and salad boxes.

Across town, when I reach it, my hostel, Backpacker Al-Katre, is welcoming. Quirky with artwork on the walls and comfy seats, I walk straight into a patio, looking up to find brightly coloured umbrellas against the sky, the colours reflecting off the windows of the first floor. The receptionist lets me put my suitcase in the cupboard until check in.

Immediately, I head off to the bus station, making the best use of my time. With my backpack heavy, crammed full of what couldn't fit in my suitcase, I stroll slowly and find the way without a map. It's very straightforward.

Once there, I buy a bus ticket to Priego de Córdoba for 8.30 am. on Thursday. I wanted to leave around 11.00 am. but there wasn't one around that time. The next one available wasn't until 1.00 pm. which is a bit late in the day, and it's a three-hour bus journey which I said I wouldn't do. Never mind, I'll just think of it as a Spanish tour rather than a long bus ride, giving me the opportunity to see lots of little villages and towns.

It means I can't go to Mezquita, however, at 8.30 am. on Thursday morning which I was hoping to do, so I'll just make sure I go tomorrow instead.

With my bus tickets sorted, I find my way back to the hostel and read my Kindle for 15 minutes until the receptionist lets me check in.

In my room, there's a top bunk, the tallest top bunk I have ever seen in all my travels, and a single bed. Luckily, mine is the single bed next to the window. Whether that's because I am here early or the lady booking me in feels sorry for me, I will never know. Either way, it's a nice surprise. The window beside my bed is open, overlooking a different patio area. It seems these houses are deceptively large.

Before I'm even settled, I go straight to the kitchen and make a cup of tea, pleased to find the kitchen is well kitted out and there's even a kettle too.

Then, taking advantage of the rest of the day, I head out to visit Palacio de Viana. It's a little complicated to find with all the tiny streets but eventually I find it, and get told there's a tour at 3.00 pm. in Spanish and that I can have a leaflet in English. Since I am not allowed around on my own, this is the only option, with 45 minutes to see the 12 patios of the palace. The first patio has a huge palm tree and the most amazing pebbled floor, it's very impressive. I love a pebbled floor and want to do one myself one day.

The gardens are divided up into areas, all flowing off one

another and each patio has a different feel to it. Some have water, most have lots of flowers. It doesn't take very long to visit them all, so when I'm done I go back and look at them all again.

Next, we step into the palace and it's immediately clear that I have drawn the short straw. While our tour guide is giving a full tour with all the facts, I have a leaflet that doesn't even tell me what room I'm in. I have to work that out by only a couple of sentences. What a waste of time.

But, all that aside, I do like it here. It's not grand as in big, the bedrooms are really small. This is more of a humble palace and the décor is warm, somewhere I could see myself living. Each room overlooks a patio, giving off a peaceful impression, and I can hear birds singing. Some huge tapestries hang on the walls, showing truly amazing amounts of skill that have gone into them, and there are some lovely rooms, well decorated but still cosy. I like it. We aren't allowed to take any photos though, which is a shame.

On coming out, I don't think it was worth the money but glad I went. I just missed a layer by not understanding Spanish.

While I am in this part of town, I visit the two churches that weren't open the other day. They might be open now but I still can't go in. I was told that I could visit any church but this one and some others have a particular emblem that I can now see on the map, saying you can only get in if you buy a ticket to the Mezquita. That's odd. Why can't I just give €1.00 and go in anyway? They turn three people away while I'm here. To be honest, by the time they explain it all to the other people in Spanish and then me in English, I see as much as I want to from the doorway, so I start my walk back and stop at a supermarket on the way to buy a courgette and onion, two oranges and another salad bowl. At the hostel, I fry my courgette and onion and it smells great – it feels so good to be cooking again. When it's done, I sit down at one of the benches and mix it all together into my salad bowl. Yummy.

Afterwards, I make a cuppa of earl grey tea from the complimentary pot and take it up to the sunny roof terrace where there are sofas and plant pots. One girl is here chilling but there's still plenty of room.

My legs are aching a bit now from all the walking. My right ankle, the one I broke years ago, is a bit painful. I don't think it likes cobbles and tiles, so I will just sit on the terrace and chill with my tea and Kindle for a while, outdoors getting some fresh air with all the chatter from the Jewish Quarter below. Birds fly by as the church bells are ringing. This will do nicely. When it gets chilly, I return to my room.

From my bedroom shutter, I watch the sky turning pink, so I go back up to the roof terrace. It's all rooftops up here but it looks like it's going to be a great sunset. I think, actually, I will go outside at street-level to see it properly instead, taking the stairs that lead from the rooftop terrace to the sleeping floor. But on my way down I miss my footing on the bend in the dark and almost fall. My life flashes in front of me. A broken foot, leg or ankle.

Thankfully, my body sorts it out and I don't fall down all the steps. What a huge relief, that could have been the end of my trip. I keep going, even though my leg and ankle hurt now, finally glimpsing the red sunset over the Mezquita as I get outside. The buildings are so mammoth here that it's difficult to see everything so I go down to the river where I see the orange and pink sky reflected across the water.

Once I've taken it all in and it grows darker, I return home, brush my teeth and get into bed. That's enough for one day.

My roommate called Simone arrives after a little while and she is a similar age to me and, even though she's Dutch, she speaks English fluently. We chat about Granada, the Alhambra, her bad luck with a credit card, and the repercussions.

After our chat, I book the hostel in Granada that she stayed in and book the Alhambra to secure it. I hadn't thought about where to stay in Granada but if she likes this hostel we are in now and recommends that one, I think we are on the same page. Plus, it's very cheap with great reviews.

Wednesday 3rd January

I slept well, even though it's as busy as you would expect in a hostel. The doors connecting the rooms to the hallway are very old and flimsy with a heavy locking system, so no one leaves their room quietly. Everyone has been to the loo and showered, complete with the sound of noisy old pipes.

Simone got up early and showered as she was off to Mezquita. I am too but not in such a hurry, it's literally a three minute walk away. I still have the headache that started last night and I'm definitely in need of a cuppa. It's either dehydration or sinus trouble, or both. Despite the tea calling to me though, I think I will just go to Mezquita and come back after.

When I get up at 7.55 am., it's still dark and, once I'm out the door of the hostel, I rush to the far end of the Mezquita, finding it full of chairs. Something is obviously going to happen here at some point today. I wasn't going to take any photos as I took loads the other day but I have to, it's just so photographic.

I wander around the edge and look at all the chapels properly. They are not huge, about 12 feet wide, and each one has its own personality and different style of decoration.

Some are gold, while others are more humble. One or two have large tapestries hanging like the ones in Viana yesterday. And a couple have the most amazing ceilings, one with intricate wooden domes, like the Alcázar in Seville. Each chapel is a beauty.

The Mezquita has evolved over the hundreds of years and I am drawn back to the oldest bit to look at the detail again. This is what is on all the fridge magnets. Beautiful stonework and carvings in the most intricate detail. I will frame one or two of these photos.

As soon as our free hour is up and Mass is about to start, the stewards ask us to leave. I'll admit, I have been thinking about going to Mass and I still haven't had much of a look at the cathedral which is huge and right in the middle, although it's sort of hidden – considering its size, that in itself is pretty amazing.

The Mass starts soon but I am not Catholic so I really shouldn't but I want to enjoy this place a bit longer, and soak up the fact that this is a religious building, spanning a complicated history with a blend of different faiths.

Suddenly, it's decided. I want to do something religious in this building; I only hope that I don't stick out like a sore thumb, get bored, or scowled upon while doing it.

It seems that Simone is going too, so we walk together into the central area that's normally fenced off, so already I know that I have made a good decision. The rows of benches face a huge, dark wood altar that is freestanding with detailed carvings so dark they are difficult to see. Framed by contrasting, delicate white and gold plaster work, the altar seems to invite us all in. The ceiling is really high, adorned with more stunning white and gold plasterwork. It's so gorgeous I can't take my eyes off it.

Soon, out come the men, five in dark pink robes, two in gold fabric, and another two in tablecloth white.

The service is special, the men's singing echoing around the cathedral, the prayers in harmony against the backdrop of church organs.

I don't understand any of it and shouldn't really be here so I don't feel totally relaxed. It is obvious to everyone that I am not Catholic because I didn't pray or go and get the rice paper, but I am enjoying it. What a beautiful setting for some beautiful words and hymns. It's a real privilege to be at a service in this wonderful cathedral inside the Mezquita.

All these things and being surrounded by them always make me question religion even more when I take part in it. Am I a worse person for not getting the rice paper, for not knowing the prayers? I don't think so. I am a good person and I am here appreciating it. I will never be Catholic but I have enjoyed this, and I am not ashamed to say it.

When the service is over, everyone else makes their way towards the exit and I see that, again, paying visitors are now allowed back in and, surprise, surprise, we are still here. It looks like we aren't going to have to leave like everyone else after all. Making the most of it, I walk around with Simone and she tells me some more history about the Mezquita that I haven't had a chance to find out yet. She points out the old parts of where we stand and how they contrast with the newer areas, which you can tell by the colour of the stone and by the fact that the ceilings are different.

I show her over to my favourite chapel which is open now, another bonus of being in here when it's open properly again. Inside, I take even more photos of the fresco painting.

At 10.40 am., over two hours later, we manage to leave.

Back at the hostel, I chat to a couple of people in the dining area, a man from India and an American lady who is living in Prague, confirming my suspicions that it's definitely more sociable in hostels. I do wonder if I messed up by not spending Christmas Day somewhere like this, but I do have very fond memories of sitting on my teal sofa drinking orange wine, and the beauty of that hotel will stay with me forever.

Soon enough though, it grows chilly. These patio houses are sort of indoors and outdoors, made so by the gaping hole in the roof.

To warm up, I brew a fresh tea and sit back down to listen to a conversation in Spanish which – thank goodness – I totally understand. But this is because one man is English and talking with no accent or rolled r's, speaking about the Mezquita and the Spanish guy beside him says that it's free if you go there at 8.30 am., like I did, and otherwise it's about €15, so I join in and tell him in English that I just went in for free too.

Listening to the English chap speak in Spanish, I'm quite amazed. If I can just learn to roll my r's like him, then understand the rolled r's and the accent, and also learn some more vocabulary, I could do this.

Saying goodbye, I head up to the rooftop where the sky is blue, warm now like a summer's day. I enjoy reading my Kindle there for a little while, then decide to explore some more and find the synagogue. The only thing left on my list.

It takes ages to find but after strolling some streets I haven't discovered yet, I eventually find it, seeing it's just one room yet with a lot of history attached to it. A plaque tells me this was built in 1315 and is the only preserved synagogue in Andalusia. I would like to learn more about the history of Córdoba and Andalusia, and might do some proper research when I get home.

By now, however, I am starving, only having had an orange so far today. The decision is whether to eat out or buy food to cook. I look at a few menus on the walls of cafés and restaurants passing by but, in the end, settle on the supermarket. I fancy eggs, they are easy to cook and will go with my half an onion and half a courgette.

First, I walk down by the river and enjoy the peace for a bit. I am done now, I think. My plan was to go to the bullfighting museum mentioned on my walking tour which, initially, I dismissed straight away. I didn't even take a photograph of it, convinced it was something ugly and barbaric, but my friend, Joanne, who is travelling around Spain at the moment, has been to the bullring in Ronda and the walking tour guide said earlier that, in the museum, you learn about the culture and why it was so important.

I consider going to enlighten myself, but I'm reminded from my research last night that the museum is read mostly in Spanish so, no, I am not going. I don't want another Viana experience where it's all in Spanish and I can't understand anything. Also, ironically the real place called Viana that I visited on my Camino is where I nearly got trapped on the streets with those huge muscular bulls. So, maybe I have had enough bull experiences. But culture is culture and that's what travel is all about, learning about these things and experiencing different situations from other people's points of view.

To coincide with my thoughts of the bulls, the horses from Seville have been on my mind a lot too. There were so many there dragging tourists about, so many of them that the streets were often soiled. There's no denying that horses have been important in every culture, that they were a means of transport for the rich and poor, that they transported people's things, were used in farming, and no one thought badly of using them then, maybe because they were essential.

Perhaps in today's life we don't need to exploit them so much, especially just for the experience of a ride around Seville. At least, that's my thoughts. But I don't know if those horses were badly treated years ago, or whether they are particularly badly treated now.

In the time I have been here in Córdoba, I am quite pleased to think I have done everything I wanted here now, and excited to move on again tomorrow, looking forward to seeing something new. I have felt at home here; luckily, it doesn't take too long before things start to feel familiar.

To me, Córdoba is patios, oranges, tiny lanes, churches, Mezquita and families.

At the hostel, I make a fried onion and courgette base, then chuck a couple of eggs on top. After eating, I bring a tea and my Kindle out to the patio area, the same one I can see from my bedroom window, and read before a man comes out to chat. He tells me he is on a Camino right now, walking from southern Spain and that, like me when I completed my own Camino, his final destination is set to be Santiago so we have lots to chat about, of course. He shares that he walked the Appalachian Trail last year too, which took him five months. From our shared experiences, we wind up talking about Grandma Gatewood, the first solo female thru-hiker who became famous for her explorations of the Appalachian Trail, and who my friend, Tami, bought me a book about to read, so I understand all about where he's been on his travels. He says he hopes to be in Santiago by March.

After a little while, my throat is getting sore again and I can feel sniffles coming on so, once I've said goodbye to my new friend, I head upstairs to bed. I won't go out anymore today and, instead, look forward to an early night ready for my long bus trip tomorrow.

Thursday 4th January

This morning, it's a struggle to get up. The bed is literally covered in scraps of tissues from where I blew my nose all night and I was probably not the best roommate. I feel bad about that.

Nevertheless, I am up and out the door in fifteen minutes, relieved I got everything ready yesterday so I can get to the bus station before it even gets light. Rain spits from the sky, streaking all the pavements wet. In my hurry, I forget that my suitcase is broken and, as I bump up a kerb, the handle comes off again in my hand, leaving the suitcase in the road. I go back and retrieve it; from now on, I will just have to lift it up the kerbs. At least it works most of the time. On reaching the bus station, I realise that I haven't drank anything since 6.00 pm. last night, probably why I have a headache to add to the mixture of dehydration and sinuses. I don't buy a drink though; I'd prefer to have a headache rather than wet my knickers on the bus. Obviously, not a good look.

By 8.35 am., we are off. The sky is overcast today so there's not much to see out of the window, only grey like Cornwall. This is not the local bus like I was expecting either. It's a coach, stopping in only five places.

Half an hour into the journey, I feel really sick and, with over two hours to go, this is not good. Suddenly I feel more urgently sick and start looking for a bag or a container, managing to throw up into the hood of my raincoat for lack of anything else available. Luckily, the coach is half empty, no one is sitting next to me and the girl across on the opposite side of the aisle is asleep. And I was quiet. I suppose I haven't eaten since 3.00 pm. yesterday so there's not much in my tummy.

After my stomach returns to normal, I feel fine, though I do wish the rest of the trip could go quickly so try to fall asleep but it doesn't work. I read my Kindle instead, carefully as screens can make me feel sick as well. To add to that, I can't let go of my raincoat hood, having pulled the drawstring in as much as I could to take care of any accidental spillage.

For the journey, I have brought a half-finished toilet roll with me and, one-handed, I blow my nose. What a blessing this coach is not full. I feel sick again and get ready to heave but it passes. Not long after, we arrive in Priego de Córdoba.

The plain bus station doesn't feel like anything special, recalling how the tourist information lady suggested here as a pretty location and, after some research, I agreed that it looked nice. But on first impressions, maybe I got it wrong. In any case, I head straight for the toilet to sort my hood out. It's so cold and damp here that I am definitely going to need my coat.

Outside, I wander a dull high street, though with the grey sky and rain falling, I'm bound to feel like pants, so it's not surprising I'm not impressed.

I buy an orange from a fruit shop and eat it while walking along the street, hoping it will quench my thirst, and hunger at the same time.

After wandering a little while, I reach my accommodation, Hospedería San Francisco, an old monastery that has been turned into a two-star hotel. Inside, it's spacious with a large open garden area in the middle, the building skirting all around.

My room, which I was expecting to be far more basic, like the convent and monasteries I visited on my Camino travels, only this one more obviously looks like a hotel room. I open the shutters and wind up the wooden blind to find I am awed by a view of mountains, right there. What a vista, it's like an oil painting.

It's so peaceful.

Settled in, I make a cup of tea with a kettle that's on the landing before going to sleep. I can't keep my eyes open any longer.

An hour later, I gather my things and a new map of the area and off I go. It's like a ghost town here though, everything is shut and the streets are empty. The one thing I remember I wanted to do here in Priego de Córdoba was to go inside the Baroque-style church, Iglesia de la Asunción, and it is shut with no information. The tourist information is also shut with no hours on the door. How disappointing.

As I keep wandering, my body tells me that I need food, and I am feeling faint now. Of the one or two bars that are actually open, they look like they only have drinks so I keep going until I eventually decide to get something from the supermarket again – then I spot a café. Thank goodness. I order a fresh orange juice rather than something fizzy, a salad which is only €4.50, and some croquettes and chips to go with it. When it all comes out it's huge, but I am in no hurry. Hopefully, the longer I stay here the more things will start opening soon. I eat as much as I can but my tummy still feels fragile.

Admitting defeat, I ask the waitress in Spanish if I can take the rest away with me, thinking I can have it for dinner later.

She takes a while, leaving me wondering if I said I was actually finished and she threw it away.

But she comes back with a carrier bag. Phew, it worked. I pay up and go to the supermarket just opposite.

There, I get two kilos of mandarins to frighten my cold away for good and some chocolate cherry sweets, like the ones I had in Ronda, as well as a tin of lentils to put over my salad, an avocado and a prepared soup since there's a microwave on the landing. This should keep me sorted for a few days.

On my way back to the hotel, I go to the tourist information, seeing it's open now, where the receptionist tells me that the baroque church will be shut for two days now. She says Mass might be on though, only I don't want to do Mass again, but if it's the only way I get in, I might do.

Back in my room, I'm dying for a cup of tea and I sip it as the view keeps changing out of the window. The mountains look clearer one minute, then a huge mist descends. It's stunning. I chill here for a while to work out what is open, and when and what I want to do here in this strange little town.

Once I'm more rested, I venture back out, finding the decorations outside are lovely, especially in a little square. There are lots more people out now and some shops are open too. I pop over to the church to find out when Mass is. I still might not be feeling great but see on the wall that Mass is at 8.00 pm. Again, joining in is not really what I want but I do want to go in.

Then, I notice the door is open ... oooh.

I step inside and see there is something happening, the place abuzz with children. I sit down quickly near the back and – would you believe it – three kings come in, practically only two minutes after me. Already, I have heard a bit about the three kings who bring the children presents on the 6th of January and it's so exciting to be part of a Spanish celebration, what's more in this beautiful church. Music plays as someone walks in singing a jolly song and the kids are all excited.

I watch it all and no one seems to care that I am a stranger, so I edge a bit nearer. The kings all sit in a row, facing the congregation, while behind them sits a big pile of wrapped presents. These kids haven't had any gifts yet, no wonder they are excited. Their names are called out and they go and each sit on a king's lap, chatting to them like you would to Father Christmas, except our children in England don't sit on laps anymore. I really shouldn't be here, but maybe I look like someone's granny with my grey hair? I enjoy the celebration even so, especially since I didn't plan any of this. I only walked over in case I could find more information.

The church is just as stunning as I thought it might be. While people take photos of their children, I take photos of the church, all white and detailed with its unusual domed ceiling.

I don't overstay my welcome, however, and leave with a smile on my face. I don't know which made me happier, getting into the church or seeing the three kings.

Friday 5th January

I'm still racked full of cold so, as soon as I wake, I eat three mandarins straight away. At least I slept well last night. With a cup of tea and some chocolate, I sit and look at the amazing view of the mountains again. Then, at 10.30 am., armed with more mandarins, a banana and my map of the town, I set off to explore Priego de Córdoba. The sky is dark and it's chilly.

The tourist information has put together a self-guided walk with 16 points of interest, so I do that. I have already got the hang of the town, as I am at the touristy end and it's all quite condensed. Starting at the tourist information, I make my way up one of my favourite streets here, wide with a lovely floor and gorgeous ornate buildings alongside filled with balconies and round windows.

When I get to the Fuente del Rey at the end of the row of majestic houses, which is the king's fountain I saw yesterday from a different angle, I admire its gorgeous stone water feature, thinking it's almost like a sculpture and a pond all rolled into one. Apparently, this fountain has 139 waterspouts, so many of them already visible.

Moving on, eventually I arrive at la Asunción church and feel so lucky to have gone in yesterday. The doors are shut but, as I walk by, a different door is open, the actual entrance. It costs €2.00 to go inside and the lady there gives me another leaflet in English. Wow, I can go in properly today instead of as an undercover grandma! The leaflet details another self-guided walk around the church and the lady says to do it in order. It's far bigger than I thought it was, even after being inside yesterday, its history going back to 1525. I walk all round and eventually come to the Sagrario which completely takes my breath away.

It's so detailed that I can't comprehend it, spanning an eight-sided room off the main church area, so bright and white. I look up at the domed roof, with its 16 segments pointing down, every other one home to a window, so there are eight windows in total on that level, high up. Below these are eight arched alcoves with windows, totalling 16 windows in all. Every surface is adorned with intricate details of figurines, flowers, patterns, scrolls. It's chaotic, and extravagant, and yet it all feels symmetrical. It's incredible.

I'm so much in awe that I have to sit down on a bench. This is possibly one of the most beautiful things I have ever seen – and I have seen some things on this trip. This is why I came to Priego de Córdoba, to see this church, and I am thrilled I have been able to witness it.

The roundness, the symmetry, the light bouncing off the white plasterwork, and the pale gold detail on the white balustrade going all the way round to form a circle; the way the gold shines with the light looks like jewels dripping. Angels grasp candlestick holders, reaching right out into the centre.

It's a work of art.

Eight angels look down from the top row of windows, making it seem like they are looking straight at me, right into my eyes, and they must be 50 feet up.

I sit on the bench for some time, not wanting to leave. I feel at home here, as if I were part of the making of it. And maybe I was. Who knows? Maybe this is why I have a love of churches and cathedrals, because I once was involved in creating one in another lifetime. I am good at crafts, I have been all my life; needlework, dressmaking, cross stitch, cardmaking, embossing, Pergamano, candle making, lace making … I have tried almost everything. At school, I was good at carpentry, and had I been a boy, I might have been a carpenter. So maybe I was involved in something like this in a past life. We will never know but I love it, and appreciate it.

Eventually, I tear myself away with a million photos to remind me of this wonderful space, and step out feeling very different to when I walked in, as if I have been coated with love. It was a privilege to enjoy that and I feel immensely privileged to be here in this funny little town, privileged that people, years ago, made such wonderful things that we can still admire.

Although I haven't come out of the church and found

religion, I have come out with a deep appreciation of the workmanship. The dreams, the skill, the love of everyone involved, almost as if I have just met them all, and can feel their enthusiasm and love for this beautiful church.

I'm very grateful it was open when I thought it was shut.

Then, just round the corner, I arrive amid some tiny lanes and now I understand why the lady in the tourist information suggested that I come here. It's gorgeous. This town just keeps giving. This area is called Barrio de la villa and it feels like I am back in Córdoba, only these lanes are exquisite, not as crowded. They are narrower, you can't see round a bed until you are there, giving the impression of feeling more intimate. The lanes meandering round, and the walls of the houses, are all painted white with loads of flowers and poinsettias on the walls. It's so photogenic, pretty and peaceful.

Even though the sky is very dark, the buildings are all glowing white, the lanes only a few feet wide in places. And there are so many flowers, from poinsettia everywhere to the geraniums. In one small space, in a tiny plaza, a Christmas tree stands. When I get closer, I realise it's not a tree at all but a carefully constructed, layer upon layer of poinsettias in the shape of a tree, red and stunning against the white houses.

A narrow lane leads me out into an open view similar to the one in my bedroom view, yet this one is more vast, spanning 180 degrees of wide countryside. It feels a little like Ronda, being on the edge of a gorge, with buildings behind and stunning, uninterrupted countryside in front. An impressive walkway leads out from here, with railings and white posts, so you can follow the edge. According to my leaflet, this is Balcón del Adarve.

The last stop, after a few more points on my walk, is the church next to me which is also impressive.

I enter through the huge door back to the monastery and slip into my room for a rest. That was quite a tour of the town and I am grateful someone put it together for people like me to enjoy. At dusk, if the weather holds or even improves – it can't quite make up its mind at the moment – apparently it will be time for the three kings, so the receptionist here told me, and I am not sure what's going to happen.

While I relax and unwind, I eat two mandarins straight away, then add lentils and avocado into my salad to bulk it out with nutrition and it tastes good.

Then, after a good rest, I go out to take part in the three kings celebrations. The problem is, I didn't get given any times for the schedule, so I just have to hope that I see something.

Out on the streets, it's very quiet and still light, so the Christmas lights aren't even on yet. I pop into the Mercador supermarket to pass the time and keep warm, buying an avocado for tomorrow and a packet of biscuits. At 5.00 pm., there's still no sign of anything and by now I need a wee, so return to my accommodation and drop my shopping off in the room.

Back outside, lots of people are wearing bright shiny clothes, I'm guessing to do with the three kings. As it gets busier, more people come from all directions, meeting in the square. There's a distinct chill around now. Above us, the lights all switch on at 6.00 pm. and people buzz about carrying cakes in big square boxes with see-through lids. I am not sure what that's about, although this tradition seems very popular. Not sure where to stand, I go into the shop to keep warm again and, in a bakery cabinet, lies a huge pile of individual cakes looking like bagels with cream in the middle, decorated with green and red bits on the top. Everyone seems to be buying them. As I wander around, I notice another lady with the same cake I have seen people carrying in the street and find them down an aisle in a long chiller. They're available in three different colours, two with cream and one without. Even though it's €5.50 and far too much cake for me, I am going to buy one anyway and celebrate properly.

I feel really chuffed coming out of the shop with my large cake, like I belong now, taking part in the celebrations that I don't know anything about. I manage to squeeze the cake in my backpack as people zoom by, mostly going left. I don't know what to do but must have picked a good spot as, suddenly, I am surrounded by families and kids who all have a bag for their sweets.

This seems to be a very social event, with everyone saying hello to whoever passes by.

I can now see lots of kids coming back with carrier bags full of sweets. They must have started at the beginning of the crowd and are now going home, or hoping to collect more. That's a lot of sweets. I still don't understand what is going on and it's very chilly now and dark. I got here about two hours early but I have to admit it's been fun watching everyone arrive.

At last, I see something. Standing up on a bench, so I can see above everyone, I have no idea what to expect, knowing only of the three kings and some sweets for the kids, that's all the clues I have. I don't need any sweets, I just want to be part of it.

The lights and noise get closer and I see it's actually a parade, when I thought it was simply going to be the appearance of three kings. Lots of floats are approaching but very, very slowly as they throw more sweets out into the crowd. So many sweets! The kids are scrabbling around to collect them all up off the floor. I pop down off my bench and even pick one up myself. I wasn't going to do that but there seems to be plenty here for everyone.

What an amazing atmosphere, chaotic and such a lot of fun. As the parade keeps going, I still don't see any kings, just lots of brightly coloured floats – and lots and lots of sweets, more than I have ever seen in one place. The parade goes on for ages, the floats great, well made, and full of adults and children dressed up in colourful outfits. I don't necessarily understand what all the floats mean. One float is bright royal blue, everyone on it wearing blue as well, with gold hats and brown painted faces. I didn't know that was a thing people did, it must represent something but I have no idea what. The floats all play loud music, clashing uproariously with each other, but everyone seems really happy.

Seeing that all the sweets are just getting squashed by the crowd, I get down off my bench and pick some more up, stuffing them into my pocket because it all only seems a waste.

Debris lies all over the road by now, filled with squashed

jellies which my feet are getting stuck to, as well as wrappers, sweet bags, and black sacks. What a mess.

Once all the floats have passed us, they turn right up the street and they're gone. That was a lot of fun. Now, I need a wind down, I want to go and photograph the tiny white lanes with the Christmas lights.

They have a different feel in the dark with decorations and lights, the streets so narrow that the lights hang easily from one side to the other while the poinsettia tree looks breath-taking.

After this, I pop back to the square to see if the floats have come back, curious to see how it all ends, and I see them coming down the last road. I might as well watch it again as I may never take part in the kings' celebration again, although I actually don't think I saw any kings.

This time watching the parade, I am on the ground, not standing on a bench, and there are hardly any children, just lots of adults. When they throw more sweets – and they really do throw them at you – I get in the groove and pick them up. I wasn't going to do it again but it's all part of the fun.

Eventually, the last float passes and there are sweets everywhere. Some people have black sacks to scoop them up, avoiding the ones just squashed to the floor. It's a bit of a waste but everyone including myself has had a good evening.

I walk home, my pocket bulging full of sweets and my cake safe in my backpack. What a crazy evening!

As soon as I get back, I make a mint tea. It's a bit late now, almost 10.00 pm., but I need to unwind and try some of this cake which I find is like sweet bread with those green and red bits on the top, and sugar crystals. It's good.

What a fun evening, one that I will remember forever.

Saturday 6th January

The sky is blue today for my last day in Priego de Córdoba. I go downstairs and bring a cup of tea back to my room and tuck into two mandarins. I am feeling much better today and add some of the kings' cake to my breakfast, sitting up in bed and ripping bits off. It's very soft before I shockingly bite into something hard. Carefully, I tear the round cake apart and inside, stuck to the dough in a tiny plastic bag, is a ceramic king. That's so cute, and such a lovely surprise. I need to find out the history of this. It reminds me of my mum cooking a Christmas pudding and putting a sixpence in it. If you found it, you would have good luck, so perhaps it's similar. And now that I have a little ceramic king about an inch high to take home as a souvenir, it's perfect.

I eat some jellies as well. I didn't realise how many I'd brought back with me but there were loads left on the floor. I could have had three times this much if I'd wanted to.

I prepare two mandarins into segments and put them in a bag, leaving at about 11.00 am. after a leisurely morning.

I head for the white lanes and take more photos as the sky is blue now, but it's actually harder to take a good photo with the sun being so strong. I record a few videos as well to try and capture it. Whatever the weather, this is one of the prettiest streets and areas that I have ever seen, and a strong competitor to Córdoba. If I could only pick one small area, this would win, although I did love Córdoba and the patios.

This is just smaller, less people, and whiter.

Just up the street is the castle which only costs €1.50 to get in, such a silly little price and a huge contrast to Seville prices.

On paying my entry, I find the castle is mostly outdoor ruins and I first go up the tower, where an exhibition a third of the way up is good to catch your breath. The tower walls and stairs are very old and worn, their history dating back to the 9th and 10th century.

For the next section, I climb a new set of stairs that have been put in place recently. They don't look like they are attached to the wall and beneath lies a big drop. My heart beats fast, finding that, after this, there's another scary climb but when I get to the top, I'm standing in a big square with a 360-degree view. I can see everything. What a beautiful day to do this, and it was all by chance. I wasn't going to come in here at all. I find my bearings and see the old monastery I am staying in and picture the roads leading to it. Mountains frame the town, while olive trees grow on many of the closer hills.

I cross the courtyard to another set of stairs, new ones that feel safe with metal ropes, and climb up to another tower where I find a tiny narrow staircase, again made of new steps but these are really deep, almost the length of my shin. I have to use my hands to help me manoeuvre my way forward as I can barely climb them.

But the view is good from the top there too, similar to the taller tower and I can see where the lanes are but not in as much detail. I can't see the gorge either. But I can sense we are near the edge of it as the buildings stop before revealing endless scenery.

Other people have come up now and I am nervous about going back down so I eat my mandarin to bide the time.

Then I must brave it. Time to go down. With no handrails and steep steps, it's a challenge, not to mention it's dark and the walls are uneven, and so old that they're jagged as I try to hold onto them for safety. I get down slowly around the bend and turn left for the next bit.

The third turret looks the same with its difficult stairs and I imagine it will be the same view, so I skip it and just wander around instead. Despite the difficulties, it's definitely been worth coming up here to get a sensation of where this town is.

When it's time to leave, I put my phone in my pocket, determined to walk away without taking a photo. However, I fail. I just want to get one more to show how steep the drop is on the edge of the gorge, to get a sense of how high up we are. Here, it does feel like Ronda but in a much smaller way, and if I weren't ill, I might've gone down to the bottom to take a photo. I just don't think I am up to it right now.

As it's such a lovely day out, I don't really want to go back but I am a little tired. Besides, I am not quite well yet and don't want to overdo it, especially as I am off to Granada tomorrow and I've already booked a walking tour for 5.00 pm.

Back in my room, at least I have the best view out of the window and later go down to heat my courgette soup in the microwave, then return to my window to eat it, along with a bit more kings' cake. It was freezing down there, which I suppose is understandable given it's a big, old stone monastery, so I switch the heating on in my room to warm up again.

It might only be 3.30 pm. but I have decided that I am not going out again today. I have seen as much as I wanted to out there and it's all been wonderful, I had no idea how lovely this town was going to be. It has everything from regal looking streets to tiny pretty lanes, a castle, lots of history, fountains, and all of it complemented by the surrounding nature, including a natural gorge and mountains.

I eat some more of my cake and find a bean that you would plant in the garden which makes me laugh. A bit of research tells me that this cake is called Rosca de Reyes, eaten on Día de Reyes, the Three Kings Day. The red and green decorations on the top represent jewels and the gifts given to Baby Jesus. If you find the king in your portion, you will have good fortune, whereas if you find the bean you have to buy the cake next year.

Watching the sun set across the mountains from my bed, eating my special cake with a cup of tea, I'm thinking how lucky I am and how much I have enjoyed Priego de Córdoba.

Sunday 7th January

The streets are still lined with sweet wrappers and cigarette ends. You rarely see many cigarette ends now in England, it's mostly all vape boxes instead.

The thermometer out here says the temperature is currently three degrees and it feels like it. By the bus stop, there are lots of late teens and early twenty-somethings standing around, a couple of parents too – they must be returning after the Christmas break.

When I climb on the bus ready to say goodbye to this sweet little town, I try to lose myself in my Kindle and, most importantly, not be sick for one and a half hours.

After such a lovely time in Priego de Córdoba, I am looking forward to staying in Granada for three days, so far only having booked the Alhambra which will complete the third important building in Andalusia. The others are in Seville and Mezquita. I didn't actually know this when I set off in December. I have learnt so much on this trip. Then there are also the lanes I didn't know about, Córdoba lanes, Priego lanes and Albaicín en Granada.

The journey is lovely, filled with more mountains in the distance and olive covered hills closer by until we pull into another bus station with a crowd waiting to get on. The driver walks up and down the aisles, counting the seats. 'Veinticinco.' Once we're moving again, the bus is rammed, everyone coughing and sneezing and it's clear I am going to need some more mandarins as soon as I get off. Eventually, out of the window, I see snow-capped mountains. They're captivating.

On arrival into Granada, it's a long walk from the station to my hostel – about 45 minutes – but at least it's good to get to know an area. My suitcase is still struggling, the handle getting weaker every time it falls off.

My first impressions of Granada are that it looks tatty. The receptionist at Priego said it was bonita. This is not bonita. Finally, I find my hostel on a narrow street with three-story buildings close to each other, so close the balconies are almost touching. A very typical Spanish street, which I loved on my Camino, but this one does feel a bit dark and unloved.

The El Granado Hostel has a good feel, nonetheless, fronted by a patio area when you walk in with a random Christmas tree decorated with baubles and a star at the top. I sense an English person's touch here. The hostel is quite plain but it does have artwork going up the stairs which is lovely and tinsel wrapped around the staircase. I retrieve the key to my bedroom and, once there, I'm greeted by two bunk beds in a small room, one on the left and one on the right with a patio door leading outside, complete with protective railing, that looks down onto a different patio area. The room might smell of feet, but my bed has a privacy curtain and a little shelf, plus it only cost €46 for three nights. I paid €40 each night in Priego, so this will balance up my spending.

A large kitchen is on the top floor with a spacious communal table. Outside, a sun terrace and three lads chilling with a guitar. Despite speaking English, none of them are from there. Meanwhile, I make a tea and soak up the sun's rays, listening to their music. This weather is so changeable, I am not sure what to wear now. It might be sunny up here but I bet it's chilly down on the street.

I leave the hostel excited and soon the sun, as predicted, disappears. At street-level, there are lots of people and I can't find my way around. My map doesn't make any sense at all.

Somehow, I get to the cathedral and find it's ginormous, so big that I can't even photograph it. I would have to step much further back but more buildings stand too close so I can't. It is seriously solid.

A tapas bar which the man on reception from the hostel recommended to me is nearby but there's a queue leading all the way outside. The other tapas bar is just the same, so I put Google Maps on and look for the nearest vegan place. It's not far. I go in and wait a few minutes for a table to be free and get shown to a tiny one amongst everyone else. They are seriously rammed in here, so much that I feel like I am sitting with people on the table to the left and the right of me.

There's no menu, just a QR code. I hate these things but can do it, only the staff have disappeared so I can't ask for Wi-Fi code. I put my data on and the screen keeps spinning up and down. It's so glitchy that I can't read much.

After a few minutes, I just get up and leave, hungry and not enjoying the environment. I google where I need to be for my walk in two hours and walk by the river in the meantime. Well, a deep ditch with very little water in it surrounded by buildings.

A lot of food places are behind curtains and a bit mysterious, while others are very expensive. I might just have to get a sandwich, though when I look in a tiny supermarket there aren't any.

I need to sit down and eat or I will be worn out before my walking tour.

Eventually, I stop at a restaurant where I like the menu, the prices, and it's outdoors. I go for a wee first – when you eat solo, this is what you have to do – then sit down but no one comes to talk to me or bring a menu. The waiter nearby only cleans tables, ignoring me.

By now, I only have one hour until my walking tour starts. It's close to here and I don't want to stress by having to find anywhere else to eat, so I go over and ask for a menu. But, with that problem solved, the waiter then doesn't come and take my order so I go back and stand in front of him and tell him what I want. It looks unnatural, he's supposed to come to my table, that's how it works. If I wasn't on a time limit, I would have already moved on.

My food arrives about 10-15 minutes later. Lasagne, because I really need something warm and hearty, and it's delicious. I was expecting a square piece on a plate with some chips but this is in a big round bowl, still bubbling from being in the oven. It's exactly what I wanted. Hot, scrummy, with lots of pasta layers, tomato sauce and cheese. I almost burn myself, it's so hot. And it was only €10. That was so satisfying.

When it's time for the walking tour, I find my man with the umbrella and have to wait another 15 minutes for everyone to arrive so I perch on a stone. A strong smell of cannabis lingers as we wait next to the pop-up traders with their shoes, t-shirts and bags all laid out on sheets. I am not feeling Granada at the moment.

However, this walk might illuminate me. It will help me decide if I want to stay an extra day or two. Or whether three is enough.

I contemplate staying in a cave, which I found out you can do here, but I am not sure I want to do that just for the sake of saying I've done it. Admittedly, that's a bit shallow. Or do I want to experience a night in a cave, just for myself?

The weather is strange again today, with the need for sunglasses and gloves. Since this tour is over two hours long, it's bound to be chilly later.

As soon as everyone arrives, we start the tour and I learn some more history of Spain. In 1492 on the 2nd of January, Granada was the last place to be taken over by Catholics, following a siege that lasted a year and a half; eventually they had to give in. Already, that has been told to me a few times but it still makes me sad. The church in front of us was once a mosque, pulled down to build a Catholic church in its place.

Our tour guide points out the river which runs under the town from this point onwards and I wonder for what reason, I love a town or city with a river running through it, why would you send it underground? Moving on, we walk through the Albaicín area which I heard is nice but, to me, it looks tatty and feels a bit unsafe. I like the narrow streets, many of them with steps as we are on a hill, so they are very photogenic. They are just not all painted white with flowers everywhere. I may have been spoiled with Priego de Córdoba.

We stop outside a museum called the Palace of the Forgotten, a museum with artifacts about torture. It's not a museum that I would want to go in and makes me feel really uncomfortable, but I suppose it's a bit like the bullring museum in Córdoba; it is part of history and culture.

Having got to the last part of my trip, I am grateful that I have learnt so much but I forget all the dates, and the kings, until all I am left with is a sense of injustice. And I hate injustice on any level.

Why anyone should be tortured for following a religion is

beyond me. I can't compute it. I can't understand how, throughout history, one religion can be totally wiped out by another.

Constantly on this trip, all the tour guides have spoken about how the Catholics pushed the Jews and Muslims out. Not only did they impose their religion on people who already had their own faith, but they knocked the mosques down, and rebuilt their own buildings.

This is horrendous and all of it has affected me. I am not religious but I am intelligent enough to know that if you follow a religion and have a faith, it is important to you. You follow certain rules, eat or don't eat certain foods, have a routine of hymns, prayers, and it's usually something that the whole family follows. You grow up with this belief system, have celebrations for different calendar events, enjoy family get-togethers, and use all this as your family foundations. I totally get all that.

So, how was it even possible for people to be told that their religion was no longer valid, that they now had to follow another one, to convert to some other religion with a completely different structure and traditions? How can you be Jewish one day, then Catholic the next? It's incomprehensible. How would these families have felt with their foundations to life stripped, and not only stripped but replaced with something completely different? I cannot understand how they coped.

And, on top of that nightmare, they were told that if they didn't convert they would be tortured.

I just can't bear it, why can't we all just tolerate each other's views? I won't be going into the museum but part of me does want to know more.

As we walk away, we are all affected and a very eloquent Muslim lady from Kuwait who is with the tour group talks in detail about what it's like to be a Muslim, including the stigma attached to it, and she is fascinating. I really enjoy the conversation between the three of us as we walk.

Next, we get to what our tour guide calls the Bill Clinton point because apparently, when Bill Clinton was here, he said this was the best sunset he had ever seen. Its official name is Mirador de San Nicolás. It's rammed with people taking photos of the Alhambra. On the skyline, the sun is setting, showing off a great view of the Alhambra sitting on top of a hill, looking very important with its snow-capped mountains behind it. The view encompasses the whole of Granada, explaining why it's so busy, especially at sunset.

After this, we venture into Sacromonte, the next area along which is the gypsy part of town where people live in caves. Some houses don't look like caves at all, however, as they are fitted with extensions to cover the entrances. We are lucky enough for the price of €1.00 each to go inside and see what a cave house looks like.

The first thing I notice is that everything is wonky, the walls, the low ceilings, and it's all whitewashed. The interiors are very humble with minimal furnishings and equipment. Shelves have been carved into the walls rather than added on.

Now I'm here, I am inspired to actually sleep in one. With the tour coming to an end, we walk back in the dark and I hope to come back and explore Sacromonte in the daylight, grateful for the tour guide sharing his experiences and knowledge of the area. He gave us lots of history and useful advice.

I wander back through town and look for a tapas bar but they are all heaving, so I look at the Christmas decorations instead which seem funny now on the 7th of January. They aren't very special, I spot another cylindrical cone. Even so, I am glad to see them. In a small supermarket, I buy one small cider and some nut mix, then return to the hostel.

Monday 8th January

In the morning, I eat two mandarins and take my flask to the kitchen on the top floor to try and socialise but it's full of men, mostly in their twenties nattering away in Spanish, so I briefly check Facebook instead before going out to explore.

Today, I want to take that iconic photo of Granada that I have seen on the internet and walk along Gran Vía de Colón, then Avenida de la Constitución, a wide path down the centre of an important road, to get there. I was told by the tour guide yesterday to turn around and I would get the view I was looking for.

Hmm. It's not like the photo that I saw. Perhaps that one must have been Photoshopped? I have to admit, it is a nice view of bustling Granada, the trees, and glimpses of snow-capped mountains, it's just not like the photo I saw.

On my way back, I see a park with a water fountain so sit down, eat my banana and look at my map.

The second thing I want to do today is wander around Sacromonte and, if I walk through the park out the other end, I will be on my way. The only snag is that it's all uphill. I climb higher and higher, yet to see any views. So far, it's just a regular street through a residential area. Every junction I get to, I keep climbing up, finding it really steep and having to stop from being out of breath. As I walk further, the view just appears, featuring more snow-capped mountains and a wide-open panoramic view down to Granada that seems so far away now. I sit on a wall, admiring the sweeping vista of the Alhambra and Granada. I have walked 9,000 steps already today.

It's busy here, full of residents driving about, getting on with life, or walking their dogs. A bit higher up, I see Michael church that the tour guide pointed out. As I have come this far, I am going to try and get to it.

I reach the old city wall, one that you can barely see from Granada but is huge when you are standing next to it. It must be 20 feet tall, if not more. A chunk of wall is missing, where they have rebuilt it in completely different brick and left a gap to walk through. The other side has an even better view of Granada and the Alhambra. Bill Clinton obviously didn't make it up here.

Granada might not be pretty but it is definitely dramatic, while the Alhambra dominates the landscape.

As soon as I reach the church, I am thrilled because this has to be the best view of Granada. I walk around the back to get a different view of the snow-capped Sierra Nevada mountains, uninterrupted by nothing but nature. It's so peaceful here. After all that, I am glad that I struggled up the hill.

I sit for a while, get my flask out and chill, letting peace wash over me, washing away the negativity I felt for Granada.

I need to be true to myself. I don't like big, busy cities with lots of roads, traffic lights and cars with people in a hurry. I need nature, and this is all a huge contrast to Priego de Córdoba.

On the way down, I walk past a row of authentic cave houses. I was told yesterday that these ones don't have electricity and water like the ones down below, truer to how the gypsies would have lived years before. A set of steps follow an old wall, leading down to a stone archway that feels very important. The wall is clearly very historic, and this must be one of the gateways. It's very peaceful here with birds singing, and home to lots of green space.

I think I am in the Albaicín area now. Although it's definitely not as pretty – the paint is falling off the walls and the floor is very uneven, the cobbles sore on my feet – it does however have some charm and history and the narrow winding streets are fun to walk around. This also completes my tour of the three important neighbourhoods in Andalusia with their signature winding streets; they are all so different.

I soon stumble across a plaza next to a building called Ayuntamiento de Granada, a lovely square with a pretty cobbled floor where lots of people eat and drink in the sunshine. It's time to sit down, so I pick a table in the sun too and order a glass of wine which arrives with my first free tapas, a small portion of very welcome paella.

This all feels very civilised, drinking wine outdoors in January with my coat and sunglasses on, and much calmer than the city. I might just sit here and drink wine and eat tapas all day.

After only one glass though, I feel a bit squiffy. When a waiter passes by, I ask him where I am on my map, and it's not where I thought I was.

After my wine and tapas, I wander the streets until I get to Sacromonte. Pretty would be the wrong word to describe somewhere like this; it doesn't look as rough as Albaicín, the walls are mainly whitewashed and it all feels less claustrophobic, the streets here being more open, layered on a hill, the buildings not as tall. It's not as tightly packed together as Albaicín either. There is less of a condensed neighbourhood feel, more in tune with nature instead as we are closer to the mountains with a clear view across the trees to the Alhambra.

I climb some steep steps to the cave museum. I have no idea how much it costs but I am sort of committed after the climb. On my arrival, I'm told it's €5.00. The lady says the Roma people who migrated here from India settled in the 15th century, and lived here up until 1963.

The whole place is home to a collection of cave houses, all obviously under the rocks with whitewashed fronts. If they hadn't been painted white, I think you would struggle to see them at all since there is hardly anything to see, the bulk of the house being inside the rock. In the centre of this community is a big space. As it's a museum now, there are lots of plaques to read and you can just wander around, going in and out of the 10 cave houses.

I first learn that the houses have been whitewashed with lime as it has lots of properties to protect the caves, one of them acting as a disinfectant which sterilises the walls and stops fungus from growing.

All around, there are many photos of the Spanish gypsies, gitano in Spanish, who used to live in these caves. The photos add something to the whole experience. The caves are all very different in size and all so wonky. They look like they have been carved by hand and that the craftsmen probably just stopped when it was practical, as soon as they reached head height. I sit down in one cave at a table and it feels really comfortable, the view out of the door across the countryside is amazing. I know it would have been hard work living in those times in a cave, but if you got on with all the other people in this little community and the kids were out the front playing, I don't think it would be too bad.

After reading another plaque, it seems that maybe I have a very unrealistic, romantic version of what life here was like. The people on this side of the huge wall were not allowed in Granada and this is where Flamenco dancing started. The plaque says that if you listen to the words in their songs, you will hear the passion and also the pain. This awakens my interest in it all, which I hadn't given much thought to before. Up until now, I have only ever seen it as a touristy element of Spain but there is obviously another historical layer to it.

There are so many viewing points of the Alhambra from Sacromonte, I realise once I leave the caves, and keep walking down through the Albaicín area until I end up at the meeting point for the walk yesterday. Was that only yesterday? Wow.

Happy with my adventures for the day so far, I turn my Wi-Fi on and look for a vegan eatery as I'm hungry again now. I find one up a street that I haven't been in before and there it is, featuring a fridgeful of pretty bowls with lots of delicious colour.

I order meatballs and two tapas but, disappointingly, only the two tapas reach me. The lady working here is obviously on her own but I think she misunderstood my Spanish.

From my tapas choices, I enjoy the paella and noodles so much that, to be honest, I'm not hungry anymore for meatballs. Maybe I will come back tomorrow after my visit to the Alhambra.

Now, with my tummy full and my mind happy after all my exploring, it's 4.40 pm. and time to go back to the hostel. First, I take a photo of this street because at the end are more snow-capped mountains, the view I was trying to get today, although it's a different street. I am glad I came this way now. I pop into a supermarket on the way back to buy food for tomorrow to take with me on my trip to the Alhambra.

As soon as I get back to the hostel, I shower straight away then make my sandwiches for tomorrow, open my one small cider can and go back to my room.

I decide, too, that if that cave house is still available to stay in overnight, I am going to book it. To my surprise, it is, so it looks like I am going to sleep in a cave on Wednesday. It will be a struggle getting my suitcase over the cobbles and up the hill, but I will work it out.

With accommodation booked for Wednesday, I then do some research about where to go next – my last destination – and book a bus ticket to Nerja on the coast. Being practical, this will get me nearer to Málaga for my flight home and it means that I don't have to stay in Málaga again on this trip. I want to save that revisit for another time; hopefully me and Phil might be able to get on a flight from Newquay for a long weekend one day.

Besides, Nerja is somewhere different to visit that I have never heard of before, plus it's by the sea which will be lovely since I have been inland for a long time since my arrival.

Now, the only thing left is to look at accommodation there. Scrolling through, it seems there's not a whole lot of choice staying within the brackets of what I want to pay, so in the end I just pick somewhere and book it. And that's it, no more accommodation to book. My trip is coming to an end.

Tuesday 9th January

Last night was unbelievable. You never quite know what is going to happen when you are in a hostel, my main thinking behind going to a hotel for Christmas.

At 2.45 am., the girl I spoke to yesterday morning on her way out to a walking tour crashed through the bedroom door. But all four of our beds were taken, so why was she here? Two new American boys were both on the top bunks and she said something to the lad, only I couldn't quite hear. Maybe they knew each other, I thought.

In her chaos, she made quite a racket. Her phone light was switched on and she was looking through the metal storage lockers, seeming a little distressed.

And all the while, I was curious, awake, and angry.

I hoped she wasn't trying to get into my locker, I thought. It was dark and I couldn't see but I wasn't about to say anything. Everything of importance was in my backpack ready for tomorrow anyway, and my waste bag was right there by my pillow. I peered round my curtain as she clattered about, needing to know what was going on. I could barely see in the dark but she was unrolling a sleeping bag and a roll mat. Was she about to sleep on the small patch of floor between the two bunk beds? Maybe the lads had sneaked her in?

Now I was really cross.

Before this, no one was snoring. With only four of us in the room, I was sound asleep and it seemed like a good night. And now I was wide awake. If I wanted to go to the loo, I would trip over her and the door probably wouldn't even open if she was in the way. Despite being in the room and laying on the floor, she still wouldn't settle. Why had she come in at 2.45 am.? Where had she been? And why was she on the floor in a sleeping bag?

At 3.01 am., finally all was quiet but I remained wide awake and, frankly, annoyed. This wasn't a kids' sleepover. I'd paid for a room with four people, not five, and there wasn't enough air for all of us with the doors and windows shut. I started rehearsing my complaint to management for the morning and it took me over an hour to get back to sleep.

I woke up at 6.00 am. when she went out to the loo and again at 7.15 am. when the two Americans left. They didn't talk to the girl which I thought was odd. But, no matter how hard I tried, I couldn't get back to sleep. It was time to get up soon too.

At 7.30 am., I turned my light on – I never usually do that but it seemed there were no rules here today. To get out of the door, I had to walk on the girl's mat and her backpack was leaning on my bed. When I came back after cleaning my teeth, she'd turned the big light on. It was clear she hadn't had much sleep either.

I had to ask. 'Why are you sleeping on the floor?'

She said someone was in her bed, the one above me. Again, odd. 'I forgot to pay for another night,' she admitted.

Ahhh. So it was her mistake. She said she'd been travelling for so long now that maybe it was time to go home and then I felt very sorry for her. She said she was going to sleep on the settee, but you can be banned if you do that. The door was open and so she came in.

From her story, it seemed like she'd spoken to someone during the day so I was left a bit confused. Why didn't she just book another night or another hostel?

Now, I know I will not be complaining about her to the hostel. She is a similar age to my daughter and albeit a bit sassy but has kept herself safe. She worked out the best thing to do under the circumstances and didn't sleep on a park bench or put herself in danger. So, I have to give her credit for that.

When I'm ready for the morning, despite the lack of sleep, I go out in search of the Alhambra for my tour there.

Stupid Google Maps sends me round in circles and squares, not seeming to work in the tall alleys, meaning I fall a bit behind on my time schedule. According to Google, it will take 38 minutes to get to the meeting point where I can gain entry which leaves me two minutes' spare. I walk faster, climbing up a hill that leads to a bend and up again onto cobbled ground. This is tough, but I have gained speed and manage to get there with ten minutes to spare. After getting the ticket, radio, and sorting out the usual passport fuss, there is plenty of time.

Off we go on our tour, it's very exciting as I have heard so much about this place over the last few weeks. What's more, it's huge, seeming more like a village perched on the top of this hill which I wasn't expecting, with lots of buildings, signposts and gardens. I am glad a tour guide is taking us around as I would probably get lost, not to mention there is a timed entrance into the palace and that would cause me a lot of stress.

We go straight into the Nasrid Palace, apparently the highlight of this tour. The walls and ceiling have all the intricate plaster work like I've seen before, however it makes it no less stunning. The summer palace is a focal point, with beautifully detailed arches that you want to keep photographing. It reminds me of lace work again from the abundance of latticed details. The more I stand here, the more I see lots of similarities to the Alcázar in Seville.

My favourite is the Hall of the Abencerrajes, its domed ceiling like a huge, stone coloured petal. The whole ceiling looks almost cave-like which sounds strange but it's so textured that it looks like it's almost dripping from above. It's quite magnificent and an awful lot of skilled people must have been involved in making this.

Another fantastic wooden ceiling is in another room, this time made of a dark wood, with a 3D, square, symmetrical effect which I love.

A trip to the dungeons is next and it's not easy hearing about the prisoners and the way they were treated. At the end is the Torre de la Vela tower that we're allowed to climb up. It's a bit of a trek but we're rewarded with a great view across Granada. This time, I can see the Albaicín neighbourhood and Sacromonte, and the huge wall that climbs up the hill, as well as the church right up the top that I visited. The guide tells us that the 2nd of January, the important day that I learned about yesterday, is a public holiday when people can get into the

Alhambra for free and ring the bell. He says, when this happens, it rings all day and can be heard from all over Granada. I love being high up here, right where the flag is. Now, when I look back from Granada, I will be able to actually see where I was standing.

Once we've climbed back down, we walk through the garden and ruins. It's probably nice here in the summer but on a grey, misty January it doesn't feel that special.

As the tour comes to an end I feel that, to be honest, I haven't learnt very much. Our guide's accent was very strong so I missed some of what he said and the group was very big. He also seemed a little bored of his job.

But I am glad that I came, it has been interesting, of course, and much bigger than I thought it would be, even though I can clearly see that it's huge from every photo that I have taken of it.

What's more, now I have been to the three important historical buildings; Seville's Alcázar, Córdoba's Mezquita and Granada's Alhambra. I am so lucky, it wasn't even something that I set out to do.

I don't think you can compare anything to the Mezquita, it's so unique, what with it being a huge mosque and a spectacular cathedral all in the same building. I think it's a stand-alone building of magnificence which I loved and would pay good money to go and visit again. Although the free session was the best because it was so quiet.

The Alcázar in Seville, in my opinion, was the most beautiful and the one I took the most photographs of because it was so stunning. It was the one that I simply stared in awe at, and more intimate, much smaller and the beauty was condensed. The gardens were also, in my opinion, much better.

The Alhambra has felt like a big, chunky defensive village on top of a hill which has some definite charm and beauty, and the most amazing views across Granada, the Albaicín and Sacromonte but, out of the three, this is the one I wouldn't return to. However, like I said, I am glad I visited. You have to see everything to compare and end up with a favourite.

I am very grateful that I have been able to visit all of them on this trip. Especially as I didn't know much about any of them when I left England a month ago.

For now, I sit on a bench in the garden here and eat my sandwich. I didn't study history an awful lot at school for some reason, so I have huge voids where knowledge should be so maybe my ignorance is showing, but I remain confused by these power takeovers. The walking tour guide said that the mosques in Granada were destroyed when the Catholics arrived, which I am still trying to get my head around. But the Alhambra is still standing. Why? Is it because it's full of wonderful buildings? Its features are obviously so Islamic and beautiful, but if it comes from another religion, the one that the Catholics fought to conquer, why is it still here?

I suppose it might be a bit strange to admire and appreciate the work of a religion that isn't your own and, no, I haven't enjoyed learning how awful humans have been to each other, often under the heading of religion, which leaves me wondering, why does religion have to be a power game? Why can't we respect each other's viewpoints and live our own lives?

To have crafted the buildings that I have seen on this trip, the Alcázar, the Mezquita, and now the Alhambra, and then to have them stolen from you, is heartbreaking. Isn't the goal for us to all get on? Then again, perhaps I am just being naive.

Sadly, it remains a fact that there is still very much wrong with the world, filled with pointless loss of life due to wars around the globe. Innocent people being killed because they are in the wrong place at the wrong time. Have we really moved on? Religion is still causing wars and innocent people are still dying. I have a lot to think about and a lot more to learn.

Although I could stay all day if I wanted to, I think it's time to leave. It's been quite an experience.

As I make my way through town, the bodegas tapas place, the one that the man on reception recommended to me, has free seats, so I sit down and order wine, along with a small soup and a tiny bit of bread as my free tapas. It's yummy.

Really, it's too cold to be sitting outdoors so, once I'm finished, I get going back to the hostel for another cuppa. The dining area is relaxing for half an hour but the few people who are here are talking to each other and, by 3.00 pm., I retreat to my room. What a shame the weather is bad, I could have sat on the roof terrace otherwise.

Sitting on my bed for an hour, I chill and read my Kindle, cosy and where I want to be. A new girl sleeps above me so I munch my three kings sweets quietly, not wanting to disturb her.

Later, I think I will eat at a different vegan restaurant this evening, one with good reviews, and I find one called Restaurant Vegano Hicuri. When I get there, the décor is amazing with fantastic artwork on the walls and my eyes absorb their full, interesting menu. I decide on a mushroom seitan and layered potato dish.

It's so good that, if I were here another day, I would come back and eat it all over again.

Outside now, it's pouring with rain. At least I have a hood, but the ground is very dangerous, the tiles being slate, or marble, and they're now wet and slippery. I try to walk very carefully, only there's so much water that it's puddling – and it's only been raining for half an hour.

As I go past the cathedral, high up is a stone gargoyle pouring rainwater noisily into the street. My feet and clothes are soaked by now but I find my way home without the map, then peel my soggy coat and trousers off before snuggling down into bed. The girl above me is possibly still asleep, though the curtains are pulled so it's difficult to say.

Once again, I read my Kindle and chill.

It's weird to think that this is my last night in a hostel on this trip. I didn't set out to stay in hostels but there is a sense of hustle and bustle that I like, the one thing missing from my stays in the hotels. It's more enjoyable being in a space with lots of different languages, where people are mostly travelling solo and interacting far more.

I have enjoyed it all, and tomorrow I will sleep in a cave.

I can't believe I'm going home soon, back to a cold caravan

and work, but the silver lining is that spring is not too far away now. I will probably be all disoriented when I return, seeing as I essentially skipped Christmas and lost a month of winter in England. It will also be good to get back to work to see my colleagues and earn some money, as no work means no pennies.

Later on during the night, I get woken up by loud voices out on the landing. I need a wee, so on my way back I investigate. It's the girl from last night, her phone is on loudspeaker and she is talking with another person in a stairwell up to the kitchen. Their conversation echoes.

I frown at her and she smiles back, she's a character.

Wednesday 10th January

All in all, I slept well. Someone new came in at midnight but settled quickly, while someone else left early but quietly.

I shower, pack, check out, and take a flask of tea with me to the patio reception area where it's chilly but at least there's a comfy chair to sink into. I can't check into my cave until 2.00 pm. anyway so there's no hurry.

At 12.17 pm., I tear myself away from my Kindle, finding it's way too cold to sit here now and look up to the sky to see it's definitely more blue than grey. These patio houses still surprise me, having the outdoors indoors.

The most stressful part of my cave sleep will be actually getting to it with my suitcase and, although I am happily more familiar with Sacromonte now, I am still getting a bus because of the cobbles. I'll aim to walk to the plaza to get the Number 34 bus to Sacromonte and then , I'll look for my cave door. How funny is that?

On the way, I pass a fruit stall and, before you know it, I have far spent too much money on fruit to eat in my cave: a persimmon, three fat medjool dates, 10 cheaper dates, and some grapes.

And to top it all off, a pomegranate because Granada means pomegranate. I admit that asking for a granada felt silly.

Moving on, I see a sign for piononos cake in a bakery that the tour guide said to try. Piononos cake is named after Pope Puis IX and this little bakery looks very traditional so I decide to buy one, costing me €1.50. While it's small, it looks authentic. Then I find my tiny bus and get on it.

I ask the driver in Spanish to take me to bus stop 39 but he says he has no idea where that is, so I just pay and sit down. He says, 'Cuevas,' and I say yes. Then he calls me over as he has found 39 on his sheet. I ask him again in Spanish to tell me when we are there. Before me, all eight seats and the two pull-downs were empty but they fill up quickly.

It's strange being in a bus looking at all the people squashed against the walls as we pass. This road is called Paseo de los Tristes which means the Promenade of the Sad, and explained on my walking tour, where they told me that this street is where funeral processions took place leading from the church to the cemetery. The guide said that the people weren't always sad because of their loss but because of the steep climb up the hill with the coffin. I don't know if he was joking or not.

This street, apparently, is one of the finest streets in Europe. I don't agree but we are all different.

Suddenly, the bus driver calls out my stop, 'Treinta nueve,' and I get off before having to climb three sets of steep cobbled steps, having to stop all the time. It's tough so I sit in an area that I have been to before on the way. I might only have half an hour before I need to check in but this is a good space to rest, a perfect lookout spot, Mirador de Mario Maya, with a magnificent view of the Alhambra. So, really, it's not difficult to sit and look across with a fresh pair of eyes, glad to know what it looks like from up here.

I can even see the flags that I took photos of yesterday by the tower and bell, when I looked across to where I am sitting now. After all my explorations, I really think I have seen Granada and the Alhambra from every possible viewpoint. More than most people do. The tour guide yesterday said we should get a taxi to the Bill Clinton Mirador. He wouldn't have believed that I walked to the top where the church is. It's bad advice saying that because, unless you are unfit or can't walk, then walking through the Albaicín is a good experience, one you are certainly not going to get in a taxi.

Two different tour guides walk by and stop right next to my bench and, while listening to them, I learn some more facts.

Here, on this side of the wall in Sacromonte, is sacred grounds where people can't be exiled; the caves are cool in summer and warm in winter; Muslims view cats as holy and admire them for their cleanliness; the name Flamenco was given in Seville when gypsy dancers from Sacromonte went to dance for money, but Flamenco itself was born in Sacromonte with the Indian gypsies who settled on this side of the wall in cave houses. Last but not least, on top of the cave houses, the owners there grow cactus to help with drainage.

Clearly, I picked a good spot to pick up some more facts.

It's good to be back in Sacromonte, I do like it here. I much prefer it to Granada, although, to be fair, I didn't do very much there, not going to any museums, and only sticking my head in the cathedral.

When I reach my cave house for the night, it has a gate reading Cueva el Duende, so I buzz until I am let in. This cave, like the others, has an extended front, so it looks like a normal house from the outside, with a gate and a small courtyard. I go through the very normal front door and down a couple of steps where a modern bathroom sits on the right. I go down a couple more steps into the cave part where there is a small, round-shaped hallway and two closed doors made of dark wood. To the right is a tiny cave-shaped kitchen area. The doors are like small church doors with arched tops.

The owner of the house says that no one is in the other room, so it's just me down here. He opens the door to my room, which is much nicer than I was expecting, and the entrance feels like it's been carved out of stone, which it has, uneven and slightly tunnel-like, and yet the room is brightly lit. The bobbly surfaces of the walls are painted white – no straight walls or ceiling here – and there's no real distinction from the ceiling or the walls at all, they simply blend together. I think I had prepared myself for a damp, cold cave but it's definitely not. It's perfect, welcoming and comfortable. There's even a Flamenco dress hanging on the wall as decoration.

The owner shows me the little kitchen area, the third area down here, but the kitchen doesn't have a door. It does, however, have a kettle. What more could I want? A plastic five-litre water bottle has a pump on the top to get the water out as there's no plumbing and then I'm shown a tiny drawer with my breakfast in it; two bits of bread wrapped in clingfilm, jam and a banana, as well as a toaster above, and a tiny table to eat at. This is all just perfect and I couldn't ask for anything more.

I put the kettle on, obviously. It's the best thing to do when you arrive in a cave for the night, then unpack my damp clothes that didn't dry yesterday as it was too cold.

The room is a very comfortable temperature, not hot or cold, just as I was told, so they might finish drying here.

While I relax, I try my strange little piononos cake, small and dumpy looking with layers of sponge in the style of a rose. It's very sweet as I was warned but it's the texture that's odd. Once I've eaten it, I am not entirely sure what it was. Soon after, I finish my tea and go out, excited to spend more time in Sacromonte.

I think a Flamenco show is a must, especially because it all originated here. That is, if it's not too late to find one. I chat to the owner outside as brings his washing in and ask about where I might see one. He tells me there are about four places to choose from.

Curious, I ask how long he has lived here, and he says 20 years, then I ask a very silly question. Does he like it? He just smiles and waves his hands at the vista with the Alhambra right there. We're standing on one of the layers of the hill that gives it a lovely open feel, with nothing in front of us but the road below, the countryside and obviously the Alhambra. He admits he doesn't like Granada either, that he prefers it here. I totally understand. So close, and yet so different.

After saying goodbye, I walk around the lanes, weaving about on different levels connected by stairs or slopes, and find a lovely spot to pause for a cold drink. A man who looks about 80 in a green parka comes over and asks what I want. I thought he was a customer, as he had his coat on, and he was sitting at a table with another elderly man chatting.

Once I tell him what I would like, he brings my drink over to the lovely sunny spot I've chosen with yet another view of the Alhambra, while chatter buzzes around me. A lady comes in and I ask her if she wants to join me as all the other tables are out of the way in the shade.

She says yes and we chat about Argentina, Brazil and Granada, her lovely moments in a museum and, after her drink, she leaves to catch a bus back to the centre. As I think of leaving too, the older gentleman who served me before brings out a triangular-shaped glass case into the eating area that he holds from the top, like a bird cage. It has three compartments and a figurine on each level, only about nine or ten inches high. He tries to take a photo of it, then comes over to me and takes the cushion off the chair opposite without saying a word, using it to frame his photo.

I want to pay my bill but this is interesting; I am in no hurry. Perhaps he made it, or perhaps it's going on eBay. He and his friend squint at the screen on his mobile and both seem chuffed with the photo. They look like great friends. He puts the glass case away inside the bar and, as he passes, I see that there's a bull and matador on each layer.

As I pay and then leave, I say, 'Gracias,' but they are too busy. This time, the man comes back out from the bar with a black Pierre Cardin bag, repeatedly saying, 'Pierre Cardin,' and numbers. I think this is going on eBay as well. The photographer takes a different cushion to use as background for this item and the two of them set it up to take a photo. I leave the entrepreneurs to it and walk away laughing.

Satisfied with my walk, I go back to my cave. I love saying that. I make another cuppa, tuck into some grapes and a few dates, before braving the pomegranate. I have no idea how to eat it, it's been a very long time since I ate one, and I even have to google it. Modern cave living with the internet.

Eating a granada in a cave in Sacromonte near Granada seems fitting. It's quite delicious but I can't remember if you eat the pips or not. I will do half and half. It reminds me of when I was a child, when my mum used to buy them occasionally as a treat. I would watch a film on a Sunday afternoon with a pomegranate because that's how long it takes to eat one.

It's 6.00 pm. now and incredibly quiet here in the cave. With no windows, anything could be happening outside, so I think I will go out for another stroll to see if there are any Flamenco shows going on and watch the sunset settling over the Alhambra.

Meandering up and down to reach the different viewpoints

is fun and I get to see the sunset with lots of different photos from different angles. It's cloudy so the sunset is amazing.

Music is coming from a tiny, humble looking house nearby. As I get closer, the door is open and I try not to be nosy but hear a guitar and just see a girl, who looks about ten, clapping along enthusiastically.

At the viewpoint near my cave home, a man bursts into song randomly, the Flamenco style music which is full of passion. I feel lucky to not only spend the night in one of these cave houses but to be here in the evening when it's a bit quieter to experience the people here too.

As I keep going, I walk carefully down the paths full of uneven stones, tempted by the lovely smells of food cooking but I am full of fruit.

Right now, I am in search of Flamenco. I can hear it but the venue from the outside says it is shut, they must be fully booked.

Instead, I find the one that the man told us about on the walking tour. Thankfully, it's open and there are people dressed up, though suddenly I'm not brave enough to go in, unable to quite make up my mind. Although I want to see the dancers, it is an expensive treat and I want to get this right.

I wander around a bit more, taking more photos of the exquisite sunset, before sitting down on a bench. These hills are tough. Meanwhile, another walking tour stops beside me.

Politely eavesdropping again, I now learn that the caves on this side of the wall were dug by people with their own hands in the 15th century, and that we only see the holes and cactus which keep the house dehydrated and free of damp, that the plants and soil keep the roofs stable so the rain doesn't wash it all away.

The tour guide says that the caves are living beings and need to breathe. If you spot a chimney on top of one, it's not for the kitchen as the residents only cook outside. It's for ventilation. The door of the cave, too, is the only contact with the outside, light only coming through when it opens. Limestone lets the cave breathe, which I already learnt a bit about at the museum.

Within the caves, it used to just be gypsies living there but now all sorts of people do, yet the caves are not cheap to buy these days.

After the group moves on, I get up and wander around again. I still don't see any more Flamenco shows open so I might be too early, though one was at 9.00 pm. which is a bit late for me. So I go back to the one mentioned on the walking tour and bravely open the door to ask about a show. The lady there says that it's starting now. It costs €28.00 here, ouch.

That price does include a drink, however, so I have sangria which seems fitting while watching Flamenco dancers performing in a cave.

In here, it's long and narrow with an arched ceiling, like one you'd find in a wine cellar. Photos hang on the walls, as well as lots of brass spoons, and a Spanish fan. It's a very intimate setting, a row of chairs along each wall with people sitting on them, and musicians sitting against the walls too. A space in the middle is dedicated for the dancers. I sit near the back as most of the chairs closer are taken already.

When the show begins, the dancers come out, their dresses more like gypsy dresses than what I originally imagined a Flamenco dancer might wear. The dresses are not flamboyant but layered and pretty with gentle ruffles that the dancers lift up as they move.

The ages of them vary – one lady looks like she's in her 70's, possibly 80's. It's difficult to say as the light is now subdued, red ones casting a subtle glow about the room.

The dancers are wonderful, so passionate and their skills are mesmerising.

The whole combination of Spanish guitars, dancers' feet tapping on the wooden floor, enthusiastic clapping from other dancers as they sit their turn, and the occasional singing, all blend together as one stunning experience.

The dancing is so rich, like an extension of each individual performer. They tug at their skirts, lifting them with one hand in time to the beats and raising the other in the air above their heads, all while tapping furiously on the boards which echoes around the cave, bouncing off the walls and wrapping around

161

us all. The dancing is telling stories as a song would but without words. I can feel the pain and emotion that they express with their faces, the tug of their dresses, the careful contained movements, each one relaying another feeling. It's so intense and almost painful. Very intimate and I feel as if their souls are dancing and the body is just carrying the history of the Flamenco.

I feel like I am witnessing something very unique. Something authentic that you couldn't learn but are born into.

At half time, all the dancers go for a break. I look at my ticket and see it reads Cuevas los Tarantos. This is the show the owner of my cave suggested, the one I couldn't find at first. The walking man recommended it as well but I always wonder whether the guides just say that because they know the owners.

It's lovely to see the place so full, you need an audience for these kinds of events.

What a good decision to come to Sacromonte, to my cave room, and to this venue.

When they come back out to perform again, the older lady dances a little slower than the others as, I imagine, the dancing must be exhausting as they move their feet so fast. But she is elegant and uses the castanets expertly, and is so expressive in her movements, as well as the expressions on her face. She has probably been dancing her whole life and this makes it even more authentic.

Then, a lot of clapping erupts and a man begins to dance. Before he starts, he seems to need the rhythm of the clapping to get him moving but soon he is so deep into the music that it feels like he is telling us a story from deep within his soul. The clapping gets stronger, his feet tap louder, and he waves his arms around, tugging on the bottom of his suit jacket as the ladies used their own clothes to express themselves. The dancer and musicians are clapping, sometimes singing with him, slowing down, then speeding up with him. There is a sense that none of this is rehearsed, that it's all free flowing and the music, dancers and singers are all blended into one.

While this dancer is not a heavy man, he is heavier with his footsteps than the females and, with it, the cave echoes. He orchestrates the music as to when to go faster, slower, and when to stop. He dances with no music at all at one point which is hypnotic, the cave is filled with the sound of his feet tapping on the wood, echoing. There seems to be music that we cannot hear but can feel it through him because he is so expressive.

This is very special. I have never seen anything like it before.

What a treat.

When it ends, I leave, glowing from the experience and I make my way through Sacromonte up to my cave house, climbing into bed feeling incredibly lucky to be here. How very lucky that I have somehow dipped myself into the history of Sacromonte.

Thursday 11th January

I slept really well. Like, solid. That could be because I have been in a noisy hostel and was catching up, or because cave living suits me.

I shower at 8.00 am. which is early for me but I don't want to miss any time in my cave, before making a cup of tea and packing. Looking around, I have made an excessive amount of mess considering how short a time I have been here. Oops. Breakfast in my tiny kitchen is wonderful, though it would have been nice if the other room had been occupied too, so I could have someone to chat to but knowing I am the only one down here is good as well. I open my little drawer and unwrap my bread before toasting it, spreading the jam over the top. The bread tastes strange, like roses, and it's very rustic and dry. The added banana and a carton of orange juice is all very kind.

Today, I can't believe I am moving on to the last destination of my trip, it seems unreal. I don't want it to end, but I do want to have a proper English meal and a decent cup of tea soon. I'm also looking forward to walking around familiar places without a map.

At 10.00 am., I need to look outside to see what the weather is like, as I have no idea if it's raining or sunny. I wonder how that would affect you long-term, being so cut off from the world.

It's silent outside except for a dog barking, and a bit chilly but the sun is shining. I sit on the bench at the top of the steps near my cave house, where I sat after arriving yesterday. Because I've had such a lovely, tranquil time here, I don't really want to leave, so I rest for a bit, taking in the vista of Sacromonte, in case I don't come back. Soon, I will need to start my journey to the bus stop.

If ever there was a place I ought to get a taxi out of, it's here. Only I don't like taxis and, besides, I'm too tight to pay for one anyway when my legs work fine, and I feel uncomfortable in them. You always have to book one and wait for it to appear, when I prefer to just walk.

And, even though it's almost an hour's walk from here to the bus station, the most challenging bit is getting out of Sacromonte with the hills, steps and cobbles, so getting a bus to town and walking the rest of the way seems like the best answer. I just need to get off the cobbles – the walk across town, I can manage.

When I'm finally ready to leave, I see that the bus only comes to the stop near my cave house every couple of hours, according to the timetable, and the other bus stop is back along the road, so I might as well walk towards town anyway. The ground is not so bobbly once I get back down on the road, but the path next to it is full of stones, albeit pretty ones, which makes it difficult with a dodgy suitcase.

I walk along 'sad road', lifting my suitcase when I need to and get back on Gran Vía de Colón, finding it easier to stick to the longer route and flat pavement rather than stagger through town across the cobbles and, quite possibly, get lost.

Soon, I reach the open-air art museum that I saw when I arrived in Granada, and have some spare time so look at the strange art and all the write-ups there, taking more photos. As I look back when I'm done, I see the snow-capped mountain in the background. I try again to get that photo that I wanted to the other day, thinking maybe I could get nearer the bus station and get a drink now too. I walk past the bronze statues and get as far as the trams.

Because, once I pass all the traffic lights to where the trams are, I reach into my pocket for my phone to take another photo but my phone is not in my pocket.

It's not in the other one. It's not in my waste bag. It's gone.

This doesn't make sense. Where is it?

I panic and almost run back over through the traffic lights, crossing unsafely before the lights suddenly change, as I drag my suitcase behind me. The three sets of lights take forever to change and every second hurts. I need to be quick and get to my phone before someone picks it up. I don't have time to stand at traffic lights! Someone might be picking it up off the ground right now. I have to get to it but the traffic is coming in thick and I can't cross the last set. Every second counts if I have dropped it.

To make matters worse, the handle suddenly falls off my bag. I finally make it back over to the path but I can't see it. Drat. I can't lose my phone.

I've been so good this whole trip, but I obviously put it in my coat pocket without clicking the popper. Now, I feel sick.

My heart beats fast. I struggle to think straight, then go back over the three sets of lights to the trams, scanning the floor, briefly scouting the roads as I cross.

But it's not there. I go back again over the lights, almost running across the roads, picking my bag up whenever the handle falls off. Did I take the last photo from the Queen Elizabeth statue? I can't remember.

I search in the bushes and look through a bin. If the cover is in there, it's definitely gone. I get back to the trams again, overwhelmed with sadness and anger at myself. You stupid woman, stupid woman! I broke my own rules of securing it every time I used it and now it's gone.

I don't want to leave. I want to keep looking. I don't want to give up hope that it's here and I will find it in a minute. I need to find it.

I stand and stare, my brain going round so fast that it's gone silent. I can't believe this is happening to me. I am so cross with myself.

But I do have to accept that it's gone. I made an error and I lost it. I tell myself it's gone, so that I can accept it and move on. But my feet don't want to leave.

Eventually, I cross the road and then stop. Where's the bus station? Oh … I was going to look on Google Maps. It's about a 15-minute walk, I think, but I don't know the way without a phone. I want to cry, this is horrible. Reality firmly sinks in.

The tears are so close that I can feel my body about to cave in and let them burst out, and rightly so. This is so distressing.

But I'm not going to cry. It's pointless, it isn't going to help and I don't have time. I can't lose it here on a street in Spain, don't want people looking at me strange or trying to talk to me in Spanish. I want to stay in control and get this sorted. I need to keep a clear head.

How am I going to find the bus station? That's my first challenge.

I start to walk in the direction I think it's in, but then stop. This is silly. I can't just guess where the bus station is, it won't be where I hope it is. I have no idea what the time might be now, perhaps about 11.00 am. and my bus is at 1.00 pm. so I do have a bit of time to work this out. A row of red buses stand over the road so I cross. A bus makes a lot of sense because it will take me to the bus station but when I get there I can't understand the timetable. I ask a bus driver who is walking by who says the 21 will take me to the bus station.

I wait as buses with different numbers come by.

Oh, no. My bus ticket to Nerja is on my phone in the app. I can't get on the bus without it. I need to find my spare phone and get it charged as soon as possible, opening my case in the middle of the street, rifling through everything. I don't care what people think.

All I can think about is that someone has my phone. Someone has it and it's my phone. They will probably flog it for €20 and I need it. It's my lifeline.

Finally, I manage to find my spare phone – thank goodness I brought one – and find the charger. Now, I need to find a socket.

I feel naked, scared and vulnerable. I have to find someone to help. I am wasting time by just waiting.

I ask two lovely old ladies which direction the bus station is in. They look horrified and say I need a bus or the metro to get there, which I don't because I walked all the way to my hostel when I arrived and have just walked here from Sacromote. I know it's not that far away but my Spanish isn't good enough to explain. They ask another lady who says the bus stop is somewhere over there, pointing somewhere else. They say the metro is a good idea. I didn't even know there was a metro in Granada. I am never going to figure that out.

Then, luckily, a number 21 bus appears. I get on it and, would you believe it, there's a charging hub onboard so I plug mine in. This could all be OK. I just need enough charge to download the Omio app to find my bus ticket.

I need to calm down. I am still stressed and my heart is beating way too fast. Soon, we arrive at the bus station. It wasn't too far but I would have struggled without a map.

I hope all my photos are backed up on Google.

This is awful. My worst nightmare. I treated myself to that phone in May and it was a big decision. I don't spend much on myself for things like phones and it's not even a year old.

I am so, so annoyed with myself.

At the bus station, I go straight in to look for a help desk but can't find one. Now, I need a wee on top of everything else too. There's a socket in the ladies, so I stand there for five minutes, only to soon realise that this isn't a good idea, I need another plan. Outside, I see a security guard and he sends me to the information desk, the one that I didn't see before because I was so stressed.

The lady behind the desk is an angel. She sees my distress, asks my name, where I am going, and prints my ticket. At last. I am getting my bus after all which is a huge relief. She tells me there's a socket to charge my phone out by the buses and I know now that I have got this, it's all going to be OK.

I'm still very annoyed with myself, and sad too, but it's alright. My phone might be gone, but at least I have a bus ticket to get to Nerja and sort it out.

I stand in the bus terminal, charging my old phone, calmer now. Holding it in my hand after owning my new one feels weird since it's a completely different weight to the one I have lost yet the cover looks like an old friend. Five minutes later, I turn it on. It says hello and turns off, so I leave it plugged in until the last minute. I need some patience.

If the bus has a charging port, it will charge for the two-hour journey.

When the bus arrives, I climb on and see that it doesn't have a charger but at least I am on it.

I realise then that I don't know the name of my hostel, and that it's on my phone in my Booking.com app. How am I going to find it without a name?

When I woke up, happy in my cave this morning, I didn't

know my day would turn out like this. But it's totally my own fault. I have a spare phone and, luckily, I packed a brand-new sim card to go with it. I just hope I can figure it out. My son, Aidan, usually helps me with these sorts of things.

I suppose you never know when things will turn good, or bad. There I was, enjoying the outdoor art gallery and by the time I was at the end of the street, it had all gone wrong.

My phone is gone. It's final. Yes or no, day or night. I either have it or I don't.

If I had known this was going to happen, I would have charged the spare phone too. I would have written the name of my hostel down.

To sort things, I could phone Phil and ask him to sign into my Booking.com but I don't know his phone number and I don't have a phone to ring him. The only number I know off by heart is my mum's. She might have his number, I am sure I gave it to her.

Thank goodness I took my Monzo card out of my phone case this morning. It's a bad habit to leave cards in your phone like that and I am grateful I had the sense to correct that this morning. Earlier, I had screenshotted the way to get to the hostel but now I don't have that either. All I know is that it's four minutes across a plaza and down a street.

I find that I can't put the new sim card into my old phone, needing one of those tiny pins to open the drawer and I don't have one. Great, this isn't going well.

I try to read my Kindle and not think about everything else.

The scenery is great coming out of Granada with more stunning snowy mountains. Very impressive. A perfect photo opportunity if you are lucky enough to have a phone.

Suddenly, sadness bubbles up inside me, as I'm staring out of the window of the bus. Someone is wandering around Granada with my phone right now. What if I don't get my photos back? My trip will be all memories. And my journal – I think that's safe, it's on Google Docs. I've had a great trip but I do love photos.

Would I have come to Spain if I had known I would lose my phone, or would I have stayed home? If you stay indoors, you will never get run over by a bus. But we have to live our lives and take the blips when they come along. As I always say, if this is the worst thing that happens, today is OK.

The scenery is so dramatic here, the road cutting through the mountains over a big bridge on stilts, sprawling over the valley below.

We pass Motril which is a strange place, unusual, and I glimpse a huge expanse of sea. It really feels like my trip is coming to an end.

If this had to happen, then it's better to have happened now rather than at the beginning of my trip. I've taken some stunning photos with the better phone and, if they are all backed up, it's going to be fine.

A niggly thought suddenly enters my head. What about my banking? Can people who have my phone gain access into my bank? Gosh, this is complicated. But I can't do anything now, I am on a bus.

We pull into Almuñécar, home to a very attractive bus stop, and the bus driver says, 'Nerja,' to people getting on. From his voice, I hear that it's pronounced Nairrka. I practise saying it correctly – if I'm staying here, I might as well learn how to say it right.

My anxiety levels rise when he opens the luggage door for the other passengers. I don't need to lose my bag as well. I stare at everyone, watching their every move in case my bag gets stolen. I will be pleased to get home so I don't have to live on my nerves anymore.

From all this, it's clear I have only made one error but it's going to have lots of repercussions.

After we get moving again, I eventually get off in a town that I have never been to before. To add to the shambles, I still have no idea where my hostel is or what it's called. How on earth am I going to find it?

I try really hard to remember the screenshots from earlier, recalling that I have to pass through a round thing with a path going through the middle, then down a straight road for something like four minutes.

I will try that. Luckily, I find the round thing easily which is a good start.

Following this, I go down the most obvious road, seeing a hostel not long after so I knock and ask if they have a reservation for me? Not unless I am called Sergio, the man laughs, as that's the only person he is expecting today.

He speaks good English and understands my situation, and even offers for me to use his office computer if it will help.

Great. That means I can go on Booking.com to find out the name of the hostel, but every password I try doesn't work and the more I try, the more my brain shuts down.

The man gets Google Maps up and calls out the hostels but they are all blurring into one. I didn't take any notice of the name when I booked it. Out of a choice of four, I just picked one.

Even though this man can't be any more helpful, I have to admit defeat and say goodbye, then walk further down the street.

One door I open actually belongs to a house, where people are eating dinner round a table as they all stare up from their plates to gawp at me. Oops. I retreat away from their door very fast.

A door to a hostel is next to theirs but no one answers. There's one over the road too, but they don't answer either. I sit on the doorstep. What am I going to do? This is such a mess.

I walk back up the street. I think I have walked more than four minutes. I will try another one.

The lady who opens the door to this hostel thinks I am asking for a room since her English is not so good. Who goes to a hostel and asks if they are booked in? You generally know where you are staying. She asks if I have booked a room with her already and I say I don't know, sounding pathetic, so she finds someone who can speak better English. Eventually, after checking her phone, she says that I don't have a room booked here.

I try another place over the road and an intercom answers, saying sorry but they are shut till next week, so it's not here.

I don't know what to do. I am running out of doors. I go

back to the square where I can hear English voices and bravely ask someone if their phone can make free calls to England.

A lady kindly lets me use her phone. I dial, waiting anxiously, but my mum is out and the call goes to the answer machine.

I can't remember her mobile off by heart, only some of the numbers. The lady then brings Booking.com up and shows me some accommodation on there. One looks like something I would book and she phones it for me, but the people on the other end think I want to book a room. This language barrier is hopeless trying to explain my situation. Then she has an idea – the waiter is bilingual, so we get him to speak to them on the phone instead. He asks my name but can't understand it, so I get my driving licence out and he calls my name out loud, even my middle name, into the phone. Everyone sitting outside at all the tables in the plaza can hear. How embarrassing.

I am not staying at that hostel. I will just have to admit defeat again and continue looking.

Down the street, I accidentally knock on the same hostel I have already been to, realising as soon as they answer the door.

To save time, I write them all down, needing to get into a system now, and head up another street, thinking maybe this will be bring me more luck. But this seems too far and they don't answer either.

As I walk, I try to remember my mum's mobile number. I turn another corner, now with no idea where I am but I do see a police station. The officers' English is as bad as my Spanish and we struggle to communicate.

They tell me I can't ring England, which I can't believe. I thought the police were supposed to help women in distress?

I am so tired and frustrated now that I don't know what to do. In the end, I go back to the square and sit down. Tears are threatening to fall again.

I honestly don't know what to do. I feel so sad. I think I have remembered my mum's mobile number now though and quickly scribble it down. I think it's in the right order, it looks right. But, of course, I don't have a phone to ring her. I might just have to book a hotel for the night, get the phone charged and go to the right place tomorrow.

I think the people on the table nearby are English. I hate asking but I have to. To my relief, they are lovely and let me ring my mum on her mobile. She says she is busy, and can I ring her back?

No, not really. Once I've explained, she tries to look on her phone for Phil's number but to do that she has to hang up. A few minutes later, she finds the number and leaves a voice message for me. We must have been ringing her in the meantime but when I listen to the voicemail message, Phil's number has only got 10 numbers in it so that doesn't work.

I ring her back to explain and she says that's all the numbers she has, so I ask her to put a message out on the group Facebook chat, resigning once more to sit and wait.

I tell Kim, the lady here who let me use her phone, that my mum is charging her iPad so we have to wait a bit to go on Facebook. I sit at the table with her and her partner, Ray, waiting.

They have an apartment here and know the area very well, meaning I get some top tips and local knowledge of the area before we have to move as the bar is shutting.

I feel awful. They probably just want to get on with their day but because their phone is my only lifeline to home, and they are kind people and we move to another bar. I feel like a stray dog they have picked up that they're not sure what to do with. I want to buy them a drink but they buy me one, a very welcome glass of wine.

Then Phil rings. Thank goodness! I ask him to go on Booking.com with my password that he keeps in our little password book and tell me the name of the hostel. He replies saying they have sent a security link to my email. What is my email password? I can't think, I could tap it into the computer without thinking about it, but under stress it just won't come to me. The brain cells in my head have been working too hard today and I don't even know my own name right now, let alone my passwords.

Kim tries to contact Booking.com to help but gets nowhere other than round in circles until Ray shows me his phone, where he has put in hostels within a four-minute walk from the bus station, clever man, and one looks a bit familiar. Kim rings it and, phew, it's my hostel. Oh my, I am so happy, so grateful.

In my excitement, I forget to ask them to let Phil know and probably don't thank them properly as I walk away, which is awful. I am just so keen to get there and to let them get on with their day. By now, the sun is setting, it's taken three hours to do that four-minute walk.

The hostel is lovely and I have a strange feeling that I knocked on this door earlier when no one answered, but I can't be sure, it's all a blur. There's no one at reception and the key is locked in the lockbox, the code to unlock it obviously sent to my phone. Luckily, I manage to find the receptionist who takes it out for me.

I plug my phone in as soon as I get to my room and go straight out. It can charge while I wander about. As soon as I reach the sea, I breathe. What a day.

From here, the sunset is gorgeous with its red streaks as I stand near Balcón de Europa, a peninsula that juts out across the sea. High up, there are walkways down below to walk by the sea, while here sprawls a large area with space to sit alongside railings to admire the views from. This looks like a lovely place; I will explore more tomorrow.

Right now, I need some food. I can't see any takeaways and don't want a restaurant, so head to Mercado and spot the hot potato dish that Tami and I had in Benidorm. Perfect. I get a bottle of cider for silly cheap money and then go home.

The phone's battery charge is on 34 percent.

I undo a staple which the lady on reception kindly gave me and try to straighten it, wiggling the tiny drawer on my phone to open it very gently, like a surgeon operating, and put the sim card in. The phone tells me I can't do anything as I'm not connected to any internet. I rush to reception where the Wi-Fi code is written on the wall, then type it in and try to buy a goodie bag with some data. It doesn't work.

I try again, and again.

Then a power cut surges right through the building. You

couldn't make this up.

I sit in the dark. How am I going to buy data with no internet?

Suddenly, the electric comes back on. I try again and it works. I am up and running.

Hooray! I am connected to the world again.

Because this is my old phone, it recognises me which means that Facebook, emails and everything is on it already, a huge bonus.

Relieved, I ring my mum and Phil who are both pleased that it's all worked out.

I look at the group chat and tell them that all is well.

Then the power goes off again.

Using my phone torch to clean my teeth, I settle down into bed, listening to Spanish men out in the corridor trying to sort the electrics out.

Friday 12th January

I am not in a hurry to get up. Yesterday was quite a day and I need to get over it. Thankfully, I slept well.

This building is called a hostel but I am not sure why because it's just like a hotel. At the top is a roof garden with a lovely open space, filled with some chairs and recliners and flags blowing in the breeze. This morning, I am in search of a kettle. I thought there was a kitchen here which was the main reason I booked it and a man on the roof garden tells me that the kettle is through the other door in the staff quarters, which used to be open to everyone. I ignore the staff signs to go and boil the kettle, having a nice chat with an English man who has been coming to Nerja for years. He tells me he has brought his granddaughter with him this time.

Heading out for a walk, I slowly make my way back to the balcony area I found yesterday and sit with a view of the sea, restaurants, and people, eating my grapes while listening to a man busking nearby. The winds are really strong here, however, so eventually I have to get up and move.

With the sea below me, I walk down a slope to find a path that meanders by the sea. After walking for an hour or so, I settle on a very nice spot to drink tea from my flask and eat a medjool date, the sweetest, softest, most delicious date I have ever eaten. Whatever it cost, it was worth it.

Feeling refreshed, I return to the hostel to make more tea and take it to the rooftop with biscuits and my Kindle for a bit. There, I chill on a sun bed where I'm happy to find that there aren't any draughts up here. Instead, it's lovely and sheltered.

After my break, I head back outside on the streets to wander and remember a bar that I wanted to visit down the steps at the balcony, a sheltered, sunny spot with no wind, right next to the beach which is perfect as I can hear the waves crashing. I order a sangria, probably my last one on this trip.

By now, and with some distance, I am OK about the

phone. Well, not OK but things go wrong in life and there's no point thinking it will be any different. When you travel, you have to expect extras, and this is my extra. I just have to absorb it and let go. I am grateful for so much on this trip. My head is bursting with images, memories and happiness. I can't be upset because, sadly, it's just one of those things. At least I brought a spare phone with me; it would have been a different story if I hadn't.

I count my cash, seeing I have €39 left. I still want to go to the caves tomorrow so hopefully I can use my card there, and I'll need a bus to Málaga on Sunday which could be paid with either cash or card. I will sort all that tomorrow.

When I have finished my drink, I sit on the beach in the sunshine. No one is swimming here, probably because the waves look rough and it's likely freezing, and I can feel myself mentally preparing to go home. I pop to the supermarket for more hot potatoes and cider on the way back to the hostel, and a couple of very small gifts as I don't have much room.

Tonight will be my last time washing clothes in the shower on this trip. I have enough clothes now till I get home. Tired, I settle down for an early night, ready for exploring caves tomorrow.

Saturday 13th January

Very nervous about finding the right train to get to the caves, I leave the hostel at 9.00 am. which turns out to be good because I go completely the wrong way at first and now I have no idea where I am. From here, I can't even see the ocean to get my bearings before I manage to work it all out. I thought there might be a queue for the first train of the day but there are only four of us on it. I chat to a lady from Bath during the journey.

I feel like a five-year-old. This is one of those open trains that chug round tourist resorts and, although it's a chilly ride, it's fun.

Once we reach our destination for the caves, I'm lucky enough to go straight in, despite booking a slot for 11.30 am. I stand there in awe. The caves are enormous, great chambers and, even though I've just stayed in one, I have never been in such a huge cave before. It's like the dome of a church, with what looks like church organ pipes dripping off the ceiling.

I can't get a feel for this size, it's just huge. A walkway leads all the way round which goes up and down stairs, making the people on the far side of the cave look tiny and the fact that all this is natural is astonishing. The whole place feels so ornate and vacuous, like the many churches and places that I have already visited on this trip, so much so that it feels like it's been purposely sculptured, and yet this is all natural. Unbelievable.

My audio guide says the central column is 32 metres tall and featured in the Guinness Book of World Records.

It also points out that some tunnel openings are high up out of reach, while beyond these are more chambers, some with the oldest drawings ever discovered on stone anywhere. Somehow, people managed to get up to that height and into another chamber which is absolutely amazing. There wouldn't have been light in here as we have now and so how on earth did they climb? It's incredible. And only skilled people go through here now with all the right equipment on.

Apparently, I learn that they burnt sticks for light.

One of the stalactites on the ceiling of this dome reminds me of fireworks falling out of the sky, frozen in stone.

It's very dry in here, including the walls. It's not like the Cheddar Gorge caves in Somerset, or the wet Mallorca caves. My audio guide says there are 30 species of creatures in this cave, some unique to here and others microscopic. How incredible, because I can't see anything at all. How did anyone even think to look for microscopic life in a cave in the first place?

I follow the walkway that clings to the edge, feeling like I'm walking around a cathedral dome. This easily compares to Alcázar in terms of intricacy and the way your eyes want to roam all over. I take some photos, knowing they won't capture a fraction of it. Partly because the camera on this phone is rubbish, partly because this is one of those things that you just can't capture.

Afterwards, I head off with the rest of the group to a VR experience in another building that's included in the price, where a huge screen stretches at about 60 feet wide. White bucket chairs also sit about two feet apart from each other, how strange. On each seat is a headset and goggles. The lady gives us instructions and says if we feel sick to close our eyes and not take our mask off.

What have I let myself in for? I thought I was watching a film about the caves.

It starts. My first thought is that Aidan would love this.

All in 3D, I am flying over the coast, Nerja below me, while the sea is behind. I can turn in my chair and look everywhere, behind and in front. It's amazing. I am flying.

Next I am in a volcano and, oh my, this is scary. Hot lava is bouncing around me before suddenly I am in a cave and it's filling up with water. It's so realistic, I think I am seeing the formation of the actual cave. It's all so real.

Now I'm flying off through tiny holes and see the artwork on the stones from the chambers that we couldn't get to earlier. I wasn't expecting to see them today and certainly not fly through the tunnel into the chamber to see them up close.

Flying high up with the cave below me is scary and exhilarating all at once as we zoom through tiny holes and I feel like I might bang my head. It's thrilling, not only that but it's teaching me so much too.

Wow.

When it ends, I feel a tiny bit sick. That was scary but I don't think I screamed.

After all that excitement, I go to the café to order some wine. I need one after that and, after all, it's the last day of my holiday.

This café has lots of windows looking out at the sea and an accompanying view of the little white village.

Well, that was 200 percent sensory overload and I still feel slightly sick, like I am flying.

I am so glad I came here. Wow, wow, wow.

From the windows outside, the sun is trying to twinkle in the sea but it's not strong enough. I breathe out, thinking I would like to do that again. It went so fast.

This place knows how to put a museum together.

Wine at 11.00 am. is foolish and extravagant, but this morning was on another level. I could stay here another hour and walk to that village on a trail but I will get the 11.30 am. bus back. Yesterday really knocked the stuffing out of me.

On the bus, I still feel a bit wobbly with emotion combined with a feeling of being utterly blessed, with tears not too far away. What a lucky girl I am. Despite the unfortunate day yesterday, I still feel incredibly grateful for all that I've experienced.

Once I'm off the bus, I go straight to the museum in the Plaza España, drinking my orange carton from the cave first to try and dilute the alcohol in my body, which I shouldn't have had but got carried away in the moment.

The museum is full of artefacts but after all I've witnessed this morning, it's a bit dry and dull.

I find somewhere for lunch where I can see the balcony area and the sea, the weather is so lovely and warm that I take my coat and scarf off while, above me, I can see green parrots squawking in the palm trees.

I order an Andalusían speciality which turns out to be egg, chips, bacon and sausage. The people who helped me first yesterday walk by and ask if I got in the hotel OK. I imagine this is an easy place to make friends.

After my meal, I move on, not wanting to take up a table for four in a prime spot for too long.

I stroll for a bit, then go back and make a cup of tea in the hostel, sitting on the roof with my Kindle on a sun bed. While I relax, I also book my bus for tomorrow online as no one was at the kiosk when I walked past on my way back.

Later on, I squeeze in one more walk along the path by the sea, collecting another potato dish from the supermarket, before returning to the balcony with my Kindle as the sun sets.

As I start to pack, we have another power cut. This one lasts ages so I just read some more in the meantime. When the power comes on again, I start packing again only to find it then switches back off. It must be time for bed now because I am shattered and probably haven't recovered physically from losing my phone yet, I have felt a bit drained ever since. It was such an emotional time, but at least I am on the last bit of my holiday and my lack of energy hasn't spoilt anything. I might have gone to Frigiliana, but I can do that another time. It's not as if I haven't already seen some stunning white villages on this trip.

However, the man next door doesn't want any of us to sleep just yet. He decides to sing, very loudly.

The people upstairs are banging on the floor but he is singing too loud so can't hear them. He sings for a good half hour and I think it's quite fitting that a drunk Spanish man should sing me to sleep, until he turns nasty, shouting at his Mrs. I have no idea what about but it soon become clear that he's one angry man. I actually feel a bit scared now he's throwing things and shouting.

Then the power goes off again. I am half prepared mentally to just leave if I have to. There might be a fire if there's an electrical fault, or if that man gets any closer I will leave. Our rooms share a little courtyard and he has his door open, just on the other side of the glass, so I feel a bit vulnerable.

The power is only off for a few minutes, however, and he storms upstairs, shouting at a different lady. Then it's all quiet for a bit. I don't know where he is.

What a crazy last night.

He's shouting again and seems even angrier now. That poor woman. I have had to deal with that in my own marriage, it's scary. He just won't let go of what's bothering him.

By 12.20 am., he doesn't sound like he's going to quieten down any time soon and he's even banging on the wall now. There's no 24-hour reception here, or this would have been sorted by now.

Gradually, it goes quiet and I can hear the shower running as his door is open again, then he storms out. I had better get some sleep before he returns.

Sunday 14th January

I have worked out the family dynamics. He has a granddaughter and a daughter on the floor above and he slept in a different room, on this floor.

That poor family.

I hate this bit, leaving the last accommodation with a day of travel ahead. But that's all part of it. I have left a big pile of rubbish again in my room, mostly potato packets from the supermarket.

It takes about an hour to get to Málaga airport and I have the usual mix of sadness that my trip has come to an end and gratitude for being able to enjoy such a trip filled with wonderful experiences. I'm also looking forward to returning to my own life and some familiarity.

Some people have commented over the last couple of years, since publishing my travel books, about the way I approach travel, surprised and occasionally frustrated by my lack of research when I travel. We all have a different life, come from different backgrounds and need different things from travel.

I need to feel free when travelling solo. I need to know that I can be spontaneous if I want to, stay an extra day somewhere, or move on. I don't research very much because I don't want to know everything about the place I am going to in minute detail. I don't want any preconceived ideas, instead preferring to do the walking tours and be inspired by them.

I think my chaotic approach to travel works for me, I have had the most amazing trip and I'm bursting with memories. It's also been thought-provoking and I learnt some important history along the way.

So, did I find Christmas? Did I change my opinion about it? Was this a good idea to just avoid it altogether?

My overriding feeling is that Christmas, for me, has definitely changed. But I have realised on this trip with more time to think, that it has always changed. It evolved over the years, slowly. From dolls and cars as gifts to computer games. From 5.00 am. starts to wondering if the teenagers were ever going to get up. Now all the children have their own lives and I should be glad. I don't have to do Christmas if I don't want to. Or I can do a new version of it.

It will never ever be what it was. Even if I am blessed with grandchildren, they won't be my children, so it won't replace what I have lost. It will be a new experience. I have to treat these feelings as a loss, and accept them for what they are.

Maybe it's a relief to be excused from Christmas. Sometimes when you go back to work after the holiday period, it's almost like a competition to see who enjoyed themselves the most. Everyone compares to see who had the best time, ate the biggest turkey, laughed the loudest, played the most games, or had the most visitors.

All my Christmases when my children were small were hard work and full of expectations but, at the heart of them, were three innocent children, eager to see what Father Christmas had brought them. The love and laughter from my children is a feeling close to my heart and this is what Christmas was, and can still be about; the love of my family.

I am surprised that I didn't feel emotional on Christmas Day. I didn't even come close. This might be because I was so far away from my children geographically, or it might be because I have come to terms with it now. Perhaps I needed to come away, step away, to realise I don't need to miss it. I certainly felt more emotional last year missing the Christmases we used to have, because I was doing a version of an English Christmas that was not what I wanted.

This Christmas wasn't really Christmas, and that's OK.

I have also come to the conclusion that to get everything that I used to love on Christmas Day, I just need to get all my children together on any day of the year, it doesn't have to be the 25th of December and it probably never will be again, but what's wrong with a random day in May, or September?

I just want to spend time with them, and I am going to concentrate on seeing them more. If I can round them all up, even better because it's not just about me seeing them, it's about them seeing each other.

The Spanish, as far as I can see, don't get very involved with the decorations, none of the shops here on my travels have been bursting with Christmas gifts, and it was very difficult in Seville to even notice that it was Christmas. It wasn't hyped and commercialised. It was like there weren't any expectations at all.

Maybe that's it. We make such a huge deal out of the 25th of December, that we have to enjoy it, have to buy lots of gifts, eat lots of food, and play games. But not everyone's Christmas is like that. The reality is that some families don't get together for whatever reason, not everyone has spare funds to be extravagant. Some families have grief to deal with at Christmas. Sometimes the expectations are too high, and we feel like we have failed if it's not like the adverts on the television.

We are supposed to love Christmas and enjoy it however, sometimes, we just don't.

I am not going to have any expectations anymore. I am not going to expect it to be great and then become disappointed, I am going to try and just go with the flow. I might even go away again over Christmas, solo or not.

We are all born with a blank page, all those pages make up chapters, and I am turning the page. I am starting a new chapter, where Christmas has evolved into something else. Not necessarily better or worse, just different and I am going to embrace it.

My advice and tips

Look carefully at flight prices and airports. Think about the additional costs. Just because a flight might be cheaper in a different town, it's going to cost you more to travel to it. You have to weigh up the expense of using a train or car parking and, depending on the flight times, possibly a hotel. It was cheaper for me to fly back to my local airport than go through the expense of a hotel and trains to Bristol.

— Keep an eye on accommodation prices. I shouldn't have spent so much over Christmas, it was a bit extravagant and those four nights at a higher budget really brought my accommodation total up. I could have saved £250 easily by staying within my usual budget. On the other hand, I did enjoy being somewhere special for Christmas.

— Join Facebook groups for the area you are travelling to and you might find some beautiful places that you would never have known about otherwise. This, for me, was Setenil de las Bodegas and Ronda.

— Use Google Maps offline. I am probably the only person who didn't know this but I am going to mention it in case only one person doesn't know. Download the area map so you can always work out where you are. This is good for walking but also for trains and buses so you know when you are near your destination.

— Get in a routine with your personal things. Have certain pockets and sections of bags for your money, phone, passport, and stick to it. If you are keeping your phone safe in a locked bag, make sure you zip it up every single time. Don't take shortcuts because that's when you lose things.

— The soup flask really saved me money. My website features a blog all about eating cheaply, so I won't detail it here.

— Get yourself a waist belt, bum bag, whatever you want to call it. A small bag that you strap to your waist to keep your phone and your money safe always comes in handy.

— Have a photo of your passport on your phone for entry to attractions and also in case you lose it.

— Bus timetables are difficult. Always speak to a human if possible. Just because you can't find a timetable online, that doesn't meant there isn't a bus. The local buses, in my experience, don't have online timetables. Look for them at the bus stops and bus stations.

— Take your old phone with you as a spare, just in case you lose your main one. It will recognise you and have all your apps. Take a spare sim card too and, if possible, a tiny pin to open the sim card drawer. Otherwise, an unravelled paperclip will do the job.

— If you leave passwords at home with someone, make sure that they can understand your scribbles and coding, otherwise it's a waste of time.

— Write the name of your next hotel you are travelling to on a piece of paper and keep this somewhere safe, not on your phone.

— I will take an extra credit card with me next time. I didn't feel comfortable putting my only card in a random cash machine.

— Some of the big attractions book up weeks to months ahead, so if you really want to go to the Alhambra or similar attractions, book them first. And check you are on a legitimate site, with good reviews.

What I won't miss
Bathrooms without windows, I hate fans.
Trying to work out how to use another shower.
Using a map every day to find your way around.
Eating badly.
Dog poop everywhere.
Tourists who don't move out of your way and don't say thank you when you do.

What I will miss
The freedom travel gives you.
New cultures.
New destinations.

What I should have packed
A cutlery set.

What I spent
Bristol, Monday 18th December 2023
Train to Western-Super-Mare – £30.59
Bus to airport – £5.00
Meal deal – £5.50
Snacks from Marks and Spencer – £5.10
Accommodation: Hathaway House, Bristol – £65.00

Málaga, Tuesday 19th December 2023
Flight to Málaga – £80.49
Bus to Málaga – £3.60
Persimmon and cucumber – 90p
Carre shop – £3.80
Hostal Larios Málaga – £36.50
Bakery – £2.20

Ronda, Wednesday 20th December 2023
Hotel Seville in Ronda – £35.65
Bus to Ronda – £13.51
Meal in a funny little café – £9.10

Biscuits – £1.10

Ronda, Thursday 21st December 2023
Hotel Seville Ronda – £35.65
Breakfast – £6.48
Ticket for tourist – £7.80
Santa María Church – £3.90
Lunch outdoors, no cutlery – £8.67
Fruit cider and chocolate from a corner shop – £4.37
Cakes in a posh shop – £1.50

Ronda, Friday 22nd December 2023
Hotel Seville Ronda – £35.65
Bus to and from Setenil – £3.67
Breakfast, gazpacho and tea – £3.90
Museum – £1.80
Keyring – £2.90
Second breakfast, two teas and toast – £2.80
Dinner by the bridge – £9.56
Cork passport holder and something for Ciara – £8.70

Seville, Saturday 23rd December 2023
Bus to Seville – £12.20
Hotel Abanico – £96.00
Food in market – £14.50
Walking tour – £8.70

Seville, Sunday 24th December 2023
Hotel Abanico – £96.00
Seville: Get your Guide to Alcázar – £22.10
Dinner: 'real food' – £15.98
Supermarket hummus and guac crisps – £3.67
Cake – £1.72
Wine on rooftop – £6.08

Seville, Christmas Day 2023
Hotel Abanico – £96.00
Tea at Hotel Alfonso – £6.00

Dinner: tapas – £9.38

Seville, Tuesday 26th December 2023
Hotel Abanico – £96.00
Cathedral/Giralda/El Salvador – £16.00
Kas – 90p

Carmona, Wednesday 27th December 2023
Convent – £30.00
Bus – £4.49
Yummy tapas in the square – £9.16
Entry to fort – £1.72

Seville, Thursday 28th December 2023
Convent (not used) – £30.00
Hostel in Seville – £17.20
Dinner – £8.74
Bus (didn't use) – £4.49
Bus – £2.90
Sangria and cake – £2.50

Córdoba, Friday 29th December 2023
Train to Córdoba – £22.74
McDonald's breakfast – £3.50
Souvenirs from Seville – £16.80
Souvenirs – £3.00
Hotel – £37.25
Salad, fizzy orange, wine, lentils, cake, savoury pasty, oat milk from Carrefour – £10.90.

Córdoba, Saturday 30th December 2023
Hotel Maestre – £37.25
Walking tour – £5.00.
Dinner – £12.45
Church Bartholomew – £2.00

Córdoba, Sunday 31st December 2023
Hotel Maestre – £37.25

Patios – £6.00
Supermarket soup and biscuits – £2.55
Tea and toast near patios – £2.50
Churros – £4.30
Burger and chips – £7.00
Cider and nuts – £2.30

Córdoba, Monday 1st January 2024
Hotel Maestre – £37.25
Ice cream – £2.50
Supermarket grapes, oranges, banana and salad bowl –
£4.28

Córdoba, Tuesday 2nd January 2024
Al-Katre hostel – £21.50
Viana entrance – £12.00.
Supermarket – £4.28

Córdoba, Wednesday 3rd January 2024
Al-Katre hostel – £21.50
Supermarket sandwich and eggs – £3.10

Priego de Córdoba, Thursday 4th January 2024
Bus to Priego – £10.61
Hotel Hospedería San Francisco – £38.30
Orange – 24p
Meal salad and croquettes – £14.30
Supermarket – £9.82

Priego de Córdoba, Friday 5th January 2024
Hotel Hospedería San Francisco – £38.30
Entrance to La Asunción church – £1.80
Supermarket avocado, miso soup, biscuits – £4.03
Supermarket cherry sweets – £2.85
Supermarket kings' cake – £4.75

Priego de Córdoba, Saturday 6th January 2024

Hotel Hospedería San Francisco – £38.30
Entrance to castle – £1.30

Granada, Sunday 7th January 2024
El Granado hostel – £13.00
Bus to Granada – £14.43
Dinner – £8.50
Walking tour – £11.00

Granada, Monday 8th January 2024
El Granado hostel – £13.00
Wine in Sacromonte – £3.50
Entrance to cave museum – £4.20
Supermarket crisps, rolls, cheese, avocado – £5.64
Supermarket cider, two guacamole pots – £4.28
Dinner in a vegan place – £5.10

Granada, Tuesday 9th January 2024
El Granado hostel – £13.00
Granada: Get your guide to Alhambra – £39.90
Wine and tapas – £3.00
Dinner in Restaurant Vegano Hicuri – £13.37

Sacromonte, Wednesday 10th January 2024
Cave house, Cueva el Duende – £43.30
Fruit – £6.10
Bus to Sacromonte – £1.20
Local cake – £1.20
Drink in café – £2.30
Flamenco dancing show at Cuevas Los Tarantos – £24.11

Nerja, Thursday 11th January 2024
Hostel Easy Nerja Bronce – £28.70
Bus to train station – £2.00
Bus to Nerja – £16.00
Supermarket food – £6.21

Nerja, Friday 12th January 2024

Hostel Easy Nerja Bronce – £28.70
Sangria – £4.90
Supermarket food – £10.10

Nerja, Saturday 13th January 2024
Hostel Easy Nerja Bronce – £28.70
Nerja caves – £18.00
Wine – £2.15
Dinner: egg and chips – £10.70
Three packets of nuts, gifts – £1.20
Supermarket potatoes – £2.15

Journey home, Sunday 14th January 2024
Bus to Málaga – £6.88
Bus to airport – £3.40
Tea at airport – £3.40
Flight to Newquay – £45.83

Extras
New phone – £219.48

Total spending
Transport – £266.03
Food – £295.91
Accommodation – £1144.95
Touristy things – £183.37
Gifts and souvenirs – £32.60
Extras (new phone) – £219 48

Total
£1922.86 for one month away.

Facebook: PaulaRooneyAuthor

Instagram: PaulaRooneyAuthor

X: @PaulaRooneyAuth

TikTok: PaulaRooneyAuthor

Printed in Great Britain
by Amazon

57996904R00116